Zen and the Art of Stand-Up Comedy

Zen and the Art of Stand-Up Comedy

Jay Sankey

Routledge/Theatre Arts Books
New York   London

Published in 1998 by
Routledge
29 West 35th Street
New York, NY 10001

Published in Great Britain by
Routledge
11 New Fetter Lane
London EC4P 4EE

Printed in the United States of America on acid-free paper.
Text Design: Debora Hilu

The cartoons "South African Piano" and "Objects in Mirror" are reprinted
by permission of *Cracked* Magazine.

Library of Congress Cataloging-in-Publication Data forthcoming

Sankey, Jay, 1963–
    Zen and the art of stand-up comedy / Jay Sankey.
        p. cm.
    ISBN 0-87830-073-2 (hb). — ISBN 0-87830-074-0 (pbk.)
    1. Stand-up comedy.   I. Title.
PN1969. C65S26 1998
792.7—dc21

                                                        97-45531
                                                            CIP

Art is science in the flesh.

—Jean Cocteau

When I'm going, when I'm really going, I feel like a jockey must feel, sitting on his horse, he's got all that speed and power underneath him and he knows, he just knows, when to let it go and how much.

—Paul Newman in *The Hustler*

At midnight I abruptly awakened. At first my mind was foggy. . . . Then all at once I was struck as though by lightning, and the next instant heaven and earth crumbled and disappeared. Instantaneously, like surging waves, a tremendous delight welled up in me, a veritable hurricane of delight, as I laughed loudly and wildly, "There's no reasoning here, no reasoning at all! Ha! Ha! Ha!" The empty sky split in two, then opened its enormous mouth and began to laugh uproariously, "Ha! Ha! Ha!"

—Koun Yamada

For Martina

Ernie for giving me a second home in Montreal

Contents

Acknowledgments

I would like to thank Bill Brownstein, Andrew Clark, Humble Howard, Daryl Jung, Shane MacDougall, Henry Mietkiewicz, Jim Slotek, and Martin Waxman for all their help promoting my stand-up shows. Thanks to David Leyes for the wonderful photographs and Ross Rumberg for the trustworthy travel arrangements. And thanks to Evan Adelman, Ed Smeall, Ann May Sirois, Jeff Silverman, and especially Mark Breslin, for the much appreciated support over the years. I would also like to thank my friends Julie Campagna, Jason Maloney, David Peck, and Tim Quinn for their kindness and patience, and my good friends and fellow comics David Acer and Barbara North for their help preparing the book. And an extra special thanks to my very dear family, Mom, Dad, Christopher, Jennifer, Gretchen, and Yashin, each of whom I continue to try to be grateful for. Finally, I would like to thank Bill Germano, Nick Syrett, and everyone else at Routledge for their belief in this book.

Introduction

This book isn't about being funny. Sure, if people laugh at something one can say, "It's funny," and if people don't laugh at something one can say, "It isn't funny." But that isn't saying a whole hell of a lot. So this isn't a book about being funny. Instead, it's a book about the *craft* involved in the performance of a particular kind of comedy, namely stand-up.

Not that I don't have some views on being funny. I do. For instance, I do not believe someone can be taught to be funny. Not from a book, not from a thirty-two-week course. Either you're funny or you aren't. But if you are a naturally funny person, I believe you can learn to be a stand-up comic. That's because, though stand-up is a kind of performance open to great art and inspiration, it is primarily a skill with general goals and guidelines. Of course, a young comic can walk on stage and ignore the principles many veteran comics swear by. In fact, it's often the daring and unconventional performers who achieve the greatest success. But for every comic that breaks the rules and succeeds, there are hundreds of comics who fall flat on their faces, giving lame performances night after night.

So though I don't believe "funny" can be taught, I do believe *stand-up can be taught to funny people*. To be a stand-up comic is to be an actor, a writer, and a director. The autonomy is wonderful, but it requires great discipline because the comic must be able to not only recognize "the funny" and write about "the funny," but also act out and deliver "the funny." Essentially, it's about developing a stand-up comic's ear, body, and voice, learning how to translate your own unique sense of humor to the stage, and paying your dues by spending hundreds of hours standing on many different stages in front of many different audiences.

There aren't a great many books written about stand-up comedy, but those I've seen often have pages and pages of jokes written by famous stand-up comics. Laughing at great jokes by professionals can be fun, but I'm not convinced it really teaches one much about stand-up comedy. It's a little like the old adage about giving people fish and only feeding them for a day, rather than teaching them how to fish and feeding them for a lifetime. Consequently, you won't find a lot of jokes in this book. Instead, this book will attempt to outline and discuss some of the guiding principles and fundamental ideas behind the writing and performance of stand-up comedy.

But there's a hitch. Because stand-up is as much an art as it is a science, I can't say the principles and ideas I'm going to discuss are cold, hard facts. Instead, they are thoughts, observations, and theories based on over twenty years of experience performing for real people, in every situation imaginable, all over the world.

Before letting you get to the first chapter, I would just like to say a few words about the *order* of the book. Words like "character," "material," and "delivery" are really just different ways of looking at the very same thing—namely, the comic and his performance. Like the four blind men who touched the elephant and arrived at four different descriptions of the animal, I too have presented the craft of stand-up from a variety of perspectives. They all describe the same thing: a public act of sharing, between an individual and a group.

For all it's apparent silliness, one person making many others laugh is no laughing matter. Especially when you consider that, sometimes the closest we can come to talking about the things that really matter to us is when we make jokes about them . . . and laugh.

Jay Sankey
Toronto, Canada
February, 1998

CHAPTER ONE

STAND-UP

Among the most remarkable features characterizing Zen, we find these: spirituality, directness of expression, disregard of conventionalism, and frequently an almost wanton delight in going astray from respectability.

—D. T. Suzuki

COMEDY AND LAUGHTER

In response to a question like "What is funny?" comics often say, "Funny is funny," and, though that doesn't say much, I would have to agree. Whatever makes someone laugh is comedy, at least to them. That's what makes laughter such a subjective and fascinating phenomenon. A person hears or sees something that strikes them as funny, and their physical system suddenly convulses, the lungs sending bursts of air out the throat, resulting in a variety of sounds, all of which we refer to as "laughter." Certainly laughter is a mysterious, highly personal response to an amazing range of things, but in my view, laughter is first and foremost *a release of tension*. Something about what the person just saw or heard (or perhaps merely thought) made him tense on an emotional or psychological level, and then something in him "chose" to release or vent this tension in the form of laughter, rather than tears or anger or some other form.

POPE AT DISNEYLAND

On a more primary, perhaps even symbolic level I'd be tempted to say that laughter is often the result of a sudden and surprising witnessing of *things either coming together or coming apart*. The magician puts a coin in his hand, then opens his hand to show that the coin has somehow vanished, suddenly breaking with the crowd's presumptions, jarring their belief in what is "real." And in response, they laugh. The comic tells a joke challenging a convention or taboo, creating tension in the crowd, and people laugh. And when the clown steps on a banana peel and takes a truly frightening fall, again we feel tension and release it in laughter. The magician, the comic, and the clown all do things that create, on some level, tension inside the audience—tension that, with the appropriate trigger, can be artfully coaxed into laughter.

WHAT IS STAND-UP COMEDY?

If I'm going to have the guts (gall?) to write an entire book about stand-up comedy, I figure I should at least give you a definition of what exactly I think stand-up comedy is. Here goes . . . Stand-up comedy is "a particular kind of performance, often given while standing on a stage in front of a microphone, during which the performer tells a scripted series of fictitious accounts in such a way as to suggest that they are unscripted, in an attempt to make an audience laugh." I know, that's quite a mouthful. Put in slightly simpler terms, stand-up comedy is telling believable lies to make people laugh.

WHY BE A STAND-UP COMIC?

Notice that the question isn't "Why *do* stand-up comedy?" That's because to a lot of comics, stand-up isn't merely something one does. It's something one is. In my case, stand-up has allowed me to rewrite my entire life and, in a sense, live a second life.

When I first began to develop my stand-up character, I was convinced I was writing about someone other than myself. But then one night onstage, it suddenly struck me that, though the *facts* of many of the jokes I tell onstage are not, strictly speaking, true about my life, the emotional themes and concerns behind my jokes are very much about who I am, what I think, and how I feel. Like in the movies, where "the names have been changed to protect the innocent," through stand-up I've been able to talk about my own odd experience of this life without losing (too many) friends or being locked up in an insane asylum. Thanks to the accepted "unreality" of anything that happens onstage, and thanks to the idea of playing a character, I've been able to both explore and express some of the strange stuff at the core of who I am, and even get paid for it!

But trying to develop and hone, not just a unique comedic perspective, but also the ability to *communicate* this perspective, takes a lot of work. And it's not really the kind of thing one can work on for just a couple of hours a day. Instead, most comics come to commit a part of themselves to it twenty-four hours a day, a part that is almost always "awake," listening to conversations, watching the world around them, and taking note of the thoughts and feelings going on inside themselves. This intensity is one of the things that makes comics so interesting, this desire to truly say what they think. In this suspicious and often "edited for television" world, the challenging comments of the stand-up comic make him a type of outspoken philosopher, an anarchist dreamer, even a kind of social hero.

STAND-UP COMICS

Never trust someone with a microphone.
—Bobcat Goldthwait

In my experience, most comics are extremely sensitive, relatively insecure, very insightful, highly intelligent people. Strong *individuals* rather than group members, with a burning desire to share what they think and feel (at least while onstage). Theirs is the perspective of the Outsider, the observer, a perspective that undoubtedly has a truth to it, but also one that is often unusually myopic. Many comics are submersed in their own seeing. This results in many fascinating imaginings and insights, but, like all things, they have their price. Comics tend to feel strangely separated from society. The odd men (and women) out. As if with them, the socialization didn't quite take.

LIFE ON THE ROAD

Making your living fully, or even partly, as a stand-up comic almost always involves travel, which usually means crappy little motels, strip malls, fast food, and a great deal of time alone in taxis, hotel rooms, and airports. Call me crazy, but I don't mind the life style. It gives me a great deal of time to write, work on my projects, go to the movies, get to the gym. And, I admit, I like room service and coming back to a magically tidied space. But there's no question that the life style can be lonely, depressing, and disorienting.

All that time on the road can also put a real strain on your relations with family and friends, which is nothing short of tragic. But many stand-ups feel what they do is closer to play than work, and in this day and age, literally running your own business, not having someone always looking over your shoulder, and only having to perform an hour a night—well, such a life style isn't going to cost nothing. Anything worth having requires sacrifice.

Comedy can be an extremely rewarding, wonderfully free form of expression, but there's no question that very few people become seasoned stand-ups without having to experience a lot of rough nights. In fact, I remember hearing someone say, "Nobody *chooses* to be a comic. It's so difficult and, at times, so amazingly unrewarding, that the only people who do it are people who don't merely *want* to do it, but for some reason, *must*."

BEING A FEMALE STAND-UP COMIC

How the hell should I know what it's like? I mean, I can't honestly say I know what it's like to be a female comic. Sure, I've thought about it a fair bit, and I've had some pretty involved conversations with female comics, but I still can't say I know exactly what it's like. But I do have some guesses.

IT WAS QUIET, TOO QUIET.

My first guess is that I wouldn't be surprised if audiences treat a female comic differently from how they treat a male comic. Second, considering that standing on a stage with a microphone in hand and deliberately trying to make people laugh at commonly held beliefs is an inherently powerful, perhaps even aggressive thing to do, and considering that our society still (!) seems more comfortable empowering men than women, I wouldn't be surprised if being a comic is a little more *complicated* for a woman than a man.

Despite the many, very funny, very gifted female comics on television, I bet some audiences, on some level, still aren't completely comfortable with a woman, onstage, making fun of stuff. How female comics deal with these differences, I do not know, but I do think it's interesting to note that, while onstage, many of the most successful female comics seem to talk more about being *human* than being *female*.

AMATEUR NIGHTS

Whether they're called "Amateur Nights," "Open Mike Nights," or "New Talent Nights," they are all basically the same thing: a performer's nightmare. Between the unbelievably bad acts, the blasé MCs, and the often cynical, doubting crowds, if you survive your time as a neophyte comic on amateur nights, I assure you, as a professional comic you will very seldom have to perform under such truly horrible conditions again. But alas, as things stand now, 99 percent of stand-up comics begin their careers by performing for weeks, months, or even years on these amateur shows.

JUST DO IT

How do you know if you can be a successful comic? There's only one way and that's to try it. You think about it and talk about it and dream about, but it's really all crap until the night you finally take a stage in front of a living, breathing crowd. So don't feed yourself lines like "I gotta write more jokes" or "I've gotta go sit in the audience another twenty times." You *literally have no idea what you're talking about.* How could you? You've never done it before!

My only advice to anyone interested in the idea of being a stand-up comic is to call up a local comedy club, ask about their amateur night, and get up on that stage. Then get off the stage, go home, and think about the experience. Then, if you like, try it again. And again. Only after you've tried it several times are you in any position whatsoever to have an opinion about what it's like to do stand-up comedy.

UNREAL AUDIENCES

Just as no two comedy clubs are exactly the same, no two clubs run their amateur nights in exactly the same fashion. They all have their own approach and feel, largely dictated by management and also by the mentality of the crowd. It's a given that a healthy percentage of the audience is made up of friends and families of the performers. Such support should certainly be appreciated, but unfortunately it also "skews the crowd," in a sense tainting the purity of the crowd's response. Yeah, it's great when your family all laugh at your stuff, but when the party of sixteen people sitting in the front row refuses to laugh at your jokes (waiting for their friend to take the stage) and then they laugh uproariously and wildly applaud at everything their friend says, well, it's all just a little unreal. Not the ideal environment to learn about what's really funny.

SADISTIC ENVIRONMENTS

Sadder still is the fact that, instead of trying to create a friendly, supportive environment in which young performers can learn, take chances, and consequently grow, some clubs encourage a kind of dog-eat-dog, Christians-at-the-Colosseum environment. In these joints, audiences are coaxed to take sadistic pleasure in watching a very frightened person break out in a cold sweat and run whimpering from the stage. I think this is not only tragic, but completely irresponsible crap. Sure, it may well appeal to some people's immature bloodlust, but with this approach, I think everyone loses in the long run.

Getting onstage is scary. Individuals exposing themselves to that extent deserve a certain amount of respect, at least as much as the amateurs bring to it themselves. By encouraging the crowd to revel in the discomfort and failure of the young performers, I believe management is merely reinforcing the prehistoric idea that comedy begins and ends with the put down. And of course, as a result, the amateurs are that much more fearful and more hesistant when it comes to taking the very kinds of risks that will yield better comics and better shows. A truly sad state of affairs.

YOUR FIRST TIME ONSTAGE

Arrive early, at least forty-five minutes before show time, introduce yourself to the MC, and find out what your position on the show is, in other words, second, seventh, thirty-eighth. Also, find out the name of the person who goes onstage just before you. Then go sit quietly in a corner and keep your eyes and ears open. There is an awful lot to learn, and the sooner you start the better. In fact, to really make the most of your time onstage you may want to consider showing up at the club a couple of hours early, just to walk up onstage, stand behind that strange, daunting microphone, and spend a few minutes looking out at the empty seats, trying to imagine they're filled with laughing people. Then get off the stage and wait as the minutes crawl by until show time.

When the show starts, watch the other acts very carefully. Yes, chances are some of them will be dreadful, but sometimes you can learn as much about a craft from someone who does it poorly as you can from someone who does it well. If nothing else, seeing really bad acts can give you some ideas about what *you shouldn't do*. When it's your turn to take the plunge, be sure to bring up a glass of water and a set list with you, have a friend push the "Record" button on your tape recorder, and walk onstage.

YOUR FIRST TEN SETS

It's a cruel fact of life that many amateurs do better their first and second time onstage than they do their fourth or fifth. The reason is quite simple. One of the keys to stand-up is to try to make everything you say look spontaneous and unrehearsed. Well, as a complete amateur, your performance is pretty close to unrehearsed to begin with! After all, having only performed once or twice, delivering your material so it looks fresh is going to be a piece of cake. One of the real challenges of stand-up—something that truly separates the men and women from the boys and girls—is the ability to deliver a joke for the *six-hundredth time* and still make it look fresh and dewey. That's a challenge indeed.

Energy is also a large factor when it comes to a successful stand-up set, and the first few times you take the stage chances are you'll be absolutely charged with energy. Granted, it's often nervous energy rather than the focused energy of a professional, but some amateurs make this nervousness work for them, not against them. However, by the fourth or fifth time onstage, as nervous as they often still are, the energy has subsided a bit, and, since they lack all the tools of a seasoned comic, their sets start to suffer. This can be very confusing, especially if you did well your first or second time onstage (and were starting to believe, like a lot of amateurs, that you were ready for your own television special).

YOUR FIRST 100 SETS

Typically, amateur comics have a boldness about them, a boldness that is essentially a reaction to their own inexperience and anxiety. Despite their bravado, deep down, most amateurs are all too aware of how little they know. Then as they learn, more often than not by having their faces rubbed in their own inexperience, they slowly become aware of just how difficult and complicated the craft of stand-up comedy can be. After nervously jumping up and down on the tightrope wire, they grow more humble as they begin to see just how far they can, in fact, fall. As a result, even if the quality of your sets suffer after your first few times onstage, in a little while you'll probably start to see an improvement, and by your twenty-fifth set, you should have a better understanding of what it's all about.

But be forewarned. You know how you thought you knew it all by your fifth set, and then realized you knew nothing? Well, that same dance tends to continue, not just for weeks or months, but years. Just when you think you've got it down . . . splat! But by your one-hundredth set, I wouldn't be surprised if you've learned some things that will actually take root, start to bloom, and stand you in good stead set after set. But remember, it takes a long time. Usually, longer than you think.

CHAPTER TWO

WRITING

Ultimately, the success of a stand-up comic is often deter-mined by his material.

—Woody Allen

To write effective stand-up material, you need three primary skills. First, the ability to develop the "comic ear," to be able to hear (and see) "the funny" in the things around you. Second, the determination to write a large quantity of jokes, the more the better. Many seasoned comics say you have to write a thousand jokes before you start to really become proficient. And third, the ability to be able to separate the good jokes from the bad. It's like panning for gold—but as a writer not only do you have to do all the panning, you also have to write the river of material! It's an awful lot of hard work, but many have done it before you. So there's no reason why you can't do it too. Just take it one joke at a time.

WHERE DO YOU GET YOUR IDEAS?

The best way to get a good idea is to get a lot of ideas.
—Roger von Oech

The question above is probably the one writers are asked more than any other. My answer is: From everywhere. Every day each of us moves through a world lush with possibilities. We are virtually surrounded by possible sparks for inspiration. But it's *seeing* them that's the hard part. What I try to do is force myself to think about stand-up as much as possible. About being onstage, about delivering my material. I also often ask myself, "What do people care about?"—a question I believe to be one of the real keys to this craft.

Good ideas sometimes just come to you, but more often than not they are the result of hard work. By "work" I mean putting energy toward putting yourself in a fertile frame of mind and giving your natural Muse the time, and the reason, to do its thing. Every successful artist has his or her own way of wooing creativity. For some, it's getting up first thing in the morning with a hot cup of coffee and a notepad, and just spending some time writing whatever comes to mind. For others, it's about always keeping a pad of paper handy when they are exercising. And then there are those who prefer to write material from deep within a hazy cloud of pricey hallucinogens. Find what works for you. Remember, it's not going to "come to you," at least not on a regular basis. You have to go to it.

THE POWER OF IDEAS

Writer's block is for amateurs.

—Charles M. Schulz

Write down every joke idea you ever have. Seriously, every single one. And don't just keep them in several different drawers all over the house (not to mention the glove compartment of your car). Go through them on a regular basis, edit them down, polish them, and even go so far as to file them, perhaps by subject, in a file system or on computer disc. Treat them like they're gold, because that's exactly what they are.

You see, unlike a comic, who is pretty much restricted to either a live performance or a television taping, a good joke idea is *raw potential* and can be used in an almost unlimited number of contexts. Commercials, album covers, posters, cartoons, radio shows, television sitcoms, plays. Ideas can freely flow from medium to medium in a way very few performers can.

Lenny Bruce kept absolutely everything, and comics who saw him perform a few years before his death say that, in his sets, they saw ideas he'd been playing with for years that had by then become much more sanded and polished. One of the really wonderful things about writing all your ideas down, and keeping them in a safe place, is that when you go over some of them several years later you'll see brand new ways of making them work onstage. If you're funny, there's probably a decent idea behind most funny thoughts you will ever have. It's just a matter of finding the right context and the right way of doing it.

So treat your ideas well. In fact, I believe ideas are not

unlike customers in a store. The better service they receive, the more likely they are to return. Remember, your ideas are precious—literally, the life blood of your craft.

THE STAND-UP EAR

With any luck (and a lot of hard work!) after performing on a few dozen amateur nights and watching many professional stand-up shows, you will begin to develop a "stand-up ear." You'll be talking with a friend on the phone and suddenly you'll hear yourself say something that sounds like a joke. Or you'll be sitting on the subway, listening to two kids talk, and again you'll hear something that sounds like a joke. With a great deal of thought and practice, both on and off stage, you will begin to hear, think, and even talk in a "stand-up sensitive fashion."

Remember, stand-up tends to focus on

1. simple ideas that can be
2. commonly understood, and
3. verbally expressed.

Subtle puns about nuclear chemistry, and party stunts that have to be performed with the lights off, do not make for strong stand-up.

EXPRESSING VS. COMMUNICATING

To me, this is one of the most important distinctions in the entire craft of stand-up comedy. When you take the stage, are you going to be a true communicator, or merely an "expressor"? Almost anyone can vent, blurt out thoughts and feelings, express themselves in one form or another. But to *communicate* is a whole other thing, because to be a communicator you have to care, not just about speaking, but also about *being heard*. That involves taking into account your audience. Their expectations, their perspectives, everything. All of which cannot help but influence material and your choice of subject, vocabulary,

IF A TREE FALLS IN THE FOREST
AND IT LANDS ON A MIME...

and speed of delivery. To be a communicator is to desire connection. Unlike the self-absorbed expressor, the communicator not only wants his audience to understand what he is trying to say, but he's willing to work to make it happen.

CLEVER VS. FUNNY

If clever is a performer balancing a pie on a stick, funny is the pie falling off and landing on the performer. I have seen some decidedly unclever comics do very well in a comedy club, and I have seen some very clever comics bomb again and again. That's because, even though most effective stand-up material has clever, witty moments, it doesn't mean people are going to think it's funny.

The difference between wit that gets belly laughs and wit that gets bored silence is not only a matter of the *style* the material is both written and delivered in, but also a matter of the *degree to which the audience cares about the subject.* An extremely clever comment about quilting is simply not going to get as many laughs as a slightly witty comment about fast food.

Now, some comics might say that, compared to jokes about quilting, jokes abut fast food are "easy," but I think this is a misguided attitude. Trying to sharpen a knife with a wet stone is certainly going to be "easier" than trying to sharpen it with a handful of butterscotch pudding. That's because, when it comes to sharpening a knife, a wet stone suits the job. In much the same way, when it comes to stand-up comedy, talking about stuff that people care about also suits the job.

ABSURDIST HUMOR

Most of the time when you tell a joke, there's something in the joke to "get." If people laugh at the joke, they got it, and if they don't laugh at the joke, they either didn't get it or they got it . . . but didn't find it funny.

But with absurdist humor, a big part of the joke is that there *isn't something to get*. The comic reaches into his pocket, removes a potato, loudly shouts, "This is a potato! It is beautiful!" and then calmly puts it back in his pocket. There's no typical pay-off—no click moment when several pieces of information suddenly come together. And it's from the very *lack* of this kind of moment, an "it all makes sense now" revelation, that absurdist humor derives much of it's tension-making potential. Absurdist humor thumbs its nose at many of the socially accepted ideas of what humor itself is. So in a sense, with absurdist humor, traditional humor itself is the victim.

As a result, doing absurdist comedy in a stand-up club can be a real uphill battle. The crowd just isn't prepared for it. Not that it can't be done; but if you are going to try it, be prepared for the crowd to need a little time to get into it. I also don't know how successful you will be if you try to *mix* absurdist humor with more traditional set-up/punchline material. After all, to an audience, what's the difference between a joke they don't get and a joke where there is nothing to get? Rather than mixing styles, I suspect you might have more success with an *entire set* made up strictly of absurdist humor. After the first few minutes, hopefully the audience will "get" that there is nothing to "get" . . . and you'll get some laughs.

I realize it may sound a little strange, thirty minutes of jokes where there is nothing really to get, but keep in mind that Monty Python did almost nothing but absurdist humor for years.

STREET JOKES

"There's these three traveling salesman, and their car breaks down near this farm. So they ask the farmer if . . ."

Almost everyone, at some time in their life, has heard a "street joke." These are jokes that pass through communities like wildfire, told from person to person, and almost always sounding vaguely familiar. That's because many of them are based on the same handful of situations, perspectives, and joke patterns. I think of street jokes as a little like prefab housing. Everything is already made, you just have to put it together. There are some people who are definitely better at telling street jokes than others, but a street joke seldom *requires* the teller to have much of a personality or perspective. He merely has to be able to convey a few pieces of information, and then try not to screw up the punchline. Most professional stand-ups avoid telling street jokes because they consider them to be too easy, common, and unoriginal, and I can't say I disagree. However, I must admit, when I've seen a comic tell a street joke in a club, the audience almost always enjoys it.

Why Should an Audience Care?

If the audience doesn't care about what you are talking about, they will not laugh. It's really that simple. No emotional investment, no fuel for laughter. Fortunately, there are several ways, both indirect and direct, to coax people to become truly involved with what you are saying.

Indirect Involvement

If people pay for something, they are often already at least a little emotionally involved. So, assuming there is a cover charge to watch the show, people will care about it and want to get their money's worth. Also, if the audience has heard positive things about a performer, either before the show or merely from the MC, they will be more apt to have positive expectations, which are another form of emotional involvement.

But there's an old saying in advertising, "The very most an advertising campaign can do is get people to try your product once. After that, it's all up to the product itself." In much the same way, paying for the show and hearing good things about you creates emotional involvement on a relatively fleeting level. No matter how much they paid or how much hype you have around you, the moment you hit the stage . . . you are on your own. That's when all the indirect means of coaxing interest come to an end, and it's time to put up or shut up. You will succeed or fail strictly on the merits of the Moment. That's why it's also essential to be able to coax interest, to get the audience to care about your performance, in a variety of ways that are both powerful and direct.

DIRECT INVOLVEMENT

People will only emotionally invest in something they care about. So if they are going to care about a stand-up performance, usually they have to care about either *what* is being said or *who* is saying it. It's you or your material, ideally both. Getting crowds to care about you, night after night, city after city, usually requires years of experience, performing for thousands of different audiences. But fortunately, getting people to care about your material is a fair bit easier. In fact, if you want to have a pretty good idea of what people care about, just open a newspaper . . . crime, drugs, violence, money, sports, education, movie stars, fitness, etc. These are the things most people care about. If you stick closely to them, you can't go too far wrong.

Ideally, you want material that *both you and the audience find funny*. If they don't find it funny, they aren't going to laugh. But if you don't find your material funny, you probably aren't going to be able to deliver with full commitment and conviction. And remember, the more deeply both you and the audience care about a topic, the more likely it will be to get a big laugh.

But as I've mentioned before, originality is an important ingredient when it comes to success as a stand-up comic. Which is why the thing you are ideally searching for is material that is not only funny to you and funny to audiences but also fresh and original.

UNIVERSAL/TIMELESS VS. LOCAL/DATED

Oddly, the more personal something is, the more universal it is as well. When we dig deeper to truthful experiences, that's the work that really touches people and connects us all.
—Bill Watterson (creator of the cartoon strip *Calvin & Hobbes*)

I bet there's a local personality in your city or town that almost everyone recognizes and knows a little about. Or something that recently happened in your area of the world that everyone is familiar with. Now, even though stuff that's familiar to everyone is exactly the kind of stuff that makes for good material, my advice to you is, if it's something or someone that only locals know about, don't waste your time writing about it.

When I first started performing on amateur nights, my goal was to make my living as a stand-up comic. And because I knew that some day, if I worked hard enough, I might get the chance to actually tour, I came up with this little guiding thought, *"Everything I try onstage must be able to play five years from now in Arizona."* To my mind, writing a joke, editing it, trying it onstage, and then polishing it over dozens of shows is hard enough as it is, without going to all the trouble for a joke that only gets laughs in my home town!

This is also one of the reasons I don't do topical humor, i.e., jokes about recent events in the news. People care a lot about what this president said or that football player did, but it gets tired and dated very quickly, and I personally am not interested in such truly fleeting information. I'd rather write material that is funny for reasons other than its topicality.

But hey, each to his own. If you want to write about

topical stuff, go to it. Lord knows many comics do very well with it. However, I would suggest that you seriously think twice about writing material that will only get laughs in your home town. I know many comics with wonderful bits that they've spent years developing that they can only perform in one or two comedy clubs in the entire world. To me, not only is that a little sad, but from a business and career perspective, it's not a very wise investment of one's time.

SURPRISE, CREDIBILITY, TRUTH, AND EXAGGERATION

As with any art, craft, or skill, there are thousands of different techniques and approaches, but certain general ideas can be suggested to be of primary importance. With stand-up comedy, the success of the material often comes down to four elements:

1. surprise
2. credibility
3. truth
4. exaggeration.

Note that these very same elements are also essential to the creation of a successful stand-up comedy character.

SURPRISE

In other words, we're back to our usual alternatives, do we
want suspense or surprise.
—Alfred Hitchcock

To me, surprise is one of the true keys, not just to keeping an audience's attention, but to comedy in general. It's
also one of the primary distinctions between jokes that
are merely witty and clever, and jokes that are gut-bust-
ing funny. A clever observation is not a joke. A witty turn
of phrase is not a joke. A joke is more a matter of *sudden,*
often ironic, insight. Surprise is the wick, it's the flashpoint,
the energy that gets the laugh "off the ground."

Imagine a weightlifter. Before he can afford the luxury
of worrying about being able to hold the weight up
above his head, he must first . . . get it there. In fact, holding the weight up is relatively easy. Getting it up there is
the hard part. That's why weightlifters put so much of
their strength behind that first lift, that initial thrust,
because to get the weight above their heads, strength is
not enough. They also need momentum. The power of
the joke's surprise often determines the initial momentum
of the audience's laugh.

CREDIBILITY

Just as it's essential for an audience to believe your character onstage, it's essential for them to believe your jokes. By
"believe" I don't mean that they must think every joke you
tell is about something that really and truly happened.
Audiences know that comics, at the very least, exaggerate.

But "suspending their disbelief" is part of their role as an audience, and most audiences are more than willing to go along with a credible fiction.

For a joke to be credible, it must be believable in two ways. It must be believable in relation to the *character*, and it must be believable in relation to the *world*. If your character is a real lady's man, telling a joke about his involvement in an orgy is believable, it makes sense. But if he says that, during the orgy, a talking llama appeared out of nowhere and started taking orders for Chinese food, the joke is no longer credible in relation to the world. The joke becomes an obvious lie. An exception to this is if the character you play onstage is himself deluded. In that case, even bizarre imaginings remain credible, because they are taken to be part of the character's own deluded idea of the real world. So when writing a joke, keep in mind that the audience must be able to *believe* that the joke suits your stage character and the world, at least as that character sees it.

TRUTH

To believe that what is true for you, is true for all men. That is genius.

—Henry David Thoreau

The truth, the way things really are. Though we all see the world in different ways, there is still a great deal we see in common. It's this stuff we have in common that we tend to call the "truth." Some comics believe this is the only stuff comics should tell jokes about. I find that a little restrictive. But there are few jokes stronger or more dependable than jokes based on everyday truths. In fact,

strictly speaking, because "truth" is more often thought of as an idea of the collective than a perception of the individual, any joke the majority of an audience laughs at must certainly contain some truth—a perception held in common.

For me, truth-based material can be divided into two categories, informational and emotional. Informational material is a joke based on a commonly known fact, for example, the fact that McDonald's restaurants have drive-thru windows. Emotional material is a joke based on a commonly held feeling, such as, that it's fun to eat food. Jokes that refer to either informational or emotional truths are often a very safe bet.

REALISTIC CABBIE I.D.

However, one of the potential dangers of telling jokes based on commonly held views is that, because the source of the subjects is common, the jokes themselves may well seem common and unoriginal. Take the fact that when a group of women are out for the night they often seem to go to the bathroom in groups rather than individually. This being a "truth," audiences will often laugh at the observation in the form of a joke, but it's also a premise that has been *done to death*. Hack. When it comes to truth-based material, the trick is to try to tap into truths that haven't been already overworked.

Exaggeration

Oddly enough, along with truth, a degree of lying is also one of the keys to comedy, namely exaggeration. Instead of saying he does his laundry once a week, the comic says he does it sixteen times. The absurdity, the obviousness of the lie, the bold fracturing of the truth can often make a crowd laugh. But realize that exaggeration often works best if it still somehow echoes the truth. If, when he says he does his laundry sixteen times a week, the comic delivers the line in such a way as to convey the sentiment "at least that's what it feels like," it will probably get a bigger laugh, because many of us can relate to the experience of dirty clothes always seeming to pile up. But, as with everything, there are limits. If the comic says he does his laundry 1,000 times a week, chances are it will not be funny, because it has no credibility whatsoever. Effective comedy is more often about stretching the truth than breaking it.

DOES EVERY JOKE HAVE A VICTIM?

Laughter is found at the debasement of your fellow Man.
—Plato

I've often thought that, if there's no corpse, there's usually no joke. If in the joke there isn't some individual, group, idea, presumption, or convention being challenged (if not butchered outright), the chances are very good it's not much of a joke. Every joke needs to have a butt. In fact, when writing material, it can often be very interesting to ask yourself, "Is there a victim in this joke? And if so, what is it?" Jokes with clearly defined victims (not unlike scripts with clearly defined characters) are often more effective than jokes with unclear victims. The victim can be almost anything. A political figure, a nearby town, someone in the audience, a chain of fast-food restaurants, even the comic himself. And sometimes the victim is simply a popular belief. For instance, if you tell a joke about something that many people think only they themselves have noticed (like how clipped toenails tend to fly through the air like boomerangs) the audience comes to realize that *everyone* experiences this, and the victim of the joke is the presumption itself, the belief that "only I experience this."

IDEAS VS. EXPERIENCES

Just as there's a difference between a crowd making an intellectual investment (understanding) and an emotional investment (caring), there is a difference between material that is idea driven, and material that is experience driven.

Jokes about strange thoughts in your head are *idea driven*, requiring the audience to use their imaginations. But jokes about your experience of going to the movies or attending a wedding are *experience driven*, requiring the audience to refer to their own, personal experience of the very same things.

Of course, many comics combine these two different approaches to material, but I think it's important, especially for a student of comedy, to be aware of the different styles, and the different appeals they make to a crowd. Incidentally, material that appeals to the common experiences of the audience tends to get laughs more often than material that asks something of the audience's imaginations. I personally think this is a rather sad commentary, but what can you do? Not that I'm suggesting you shouldn't bother to challenge people's imaginations (only doing jokes about how women love to shop and how kids who work in fast-food restaurants always have facial blemishes). But I do think it's a good idea, before going in front of yet another audience, at least to be aware of such tendencies.

WHAT IS A JOKE?

Humor often makes light of heavy things (a joke about Jesus on the Cross) or "makes heavy" of light things (getting extremely upset about a missing shirt button), and this often involves at least some exaggeration or distortion. But the vast majority of jokes seem to involve, first, the communicating of a small amount of information and, second, a final piece of information that yields *a sudden shifting of perception*. The initially given small amount of information is what comics call the "set-up," and the final piece of information, the "punchline."

SET-UPS AND PUNCHLINES

Most jokes are made up of two parts: the *set-up* and the *punchline*. Curiosity and surprise, tension and release. Some comics present these pairings in a very simple, direct, and bold fashion, so that the audience can almost guess exactly when the punchline is coming. Other comics camouflage this underlying set-up/punchline structure, both with their delivery and their writing, presenting their material in a more subtle fashion. But make no mistake. This set-up/punchline structure is behind 99 percent of the comedy you will ever see getting laughs on a stand-up stage.

SET-UPS

A set-up is the information the comic gives to the crowd *to establish an initial subject, context, and perspective*. I know, sounds pretty abstract. Instead, imagine the comic taking a lovely colored balloon out of his pocket and slowly blowing it up. This is exactly like an effective set-up. Well-written set-ups do several things. They both appeal to and engage the crowd, making people want to listen to what you are talking about. They also make the audience curious, piquing their interest and sparking their imaginations. And finally, a good set-up also creates, on some level, a subtle (and sometimes not so subtle) tension in the audience. All of which, again, is not unlike the blowing up of a balloon. Here's a set-up . . .

AGORAPHOBIC   ANGORAPHOBIC

"I knew a girl in Grade 5 who had a sixth finger on her right hand . . .

PUNCHLINES

A punchline is the final information the comic gives to the crowd; *it alters the meaning of already given information in a surprising fashion.* Again, pretty abstract. But if a good set-up is like the comic blowing up a balloon, a good punchline is the pin the comic suddenly produces to burst the balloon. Well-written punchlines are not so much about engaging the crowd or appealing to curiosity.

Effective punchlines are more about surprise, irony, brevity, and imagination. A punchline shouldn't just tap the crowd on the shoulder, it should be more like a shovel to the back of the head (however gently wielded). Effective punchlines are often a single sentence, as short as possible, that dramatically changes the meaning, spirit, or direction of the joke, while giving any built-up tension a sudden and completely unexpected opportunity for *release*. Very much like the sudden bursting of a lovely balloon. Here's the punchline to the joke about the girl with a sixth-finger. . .

> ". . . it looked pretty strange. But she was the school 'scissors, paper, rock' champ."

TAGS

I know I said jokes are usually made-up of two parts, and believe me, I was telling the truth. But there's a third part to many jokes, especially jokes told by professional comics. This part is called the "tag." A tag is a brief funny line, said after the audience has laughed at the punchline. It isn't so much another punchline as it is additional information in relation to the just-delivered punchline. Here's a tag to the sixth-finger joke . . .

> "Oh oh, here she comes now. Better put away your milk money."

CLICK MOMENTS

To me, this is pretty much *the key to stand-up comedy*. Effective jokes tend to have at least one single, clear moment, usually at the end of the punchline, where the listener experiences already given information suddenly coming together in a surprising fashion, due to one last piece of information. I think of this funny realization as a "click moment," a moment where all the information in the joke suddenly "clicks" together. Generally speaking, the more suddenly and clearly the comic communicates this last piece in the puzzle, the more powerful the click moment and the louder the laugh. Like many young comics, during my first couple of years I wrote many things that I *thought* were jokes, but as clever or witty or insightful as they may have been, all too often they lacked a *clearly defined click moment.*

Think of this moment as a surprising, sharp change in the direction of the information the comic is giving to the audience. Up until this moment, the comic is speaking in a very plain and straightforward fashion. But with a click moment, the seemingly straight is suddenly revealed to be in fact bent, an acute corner appearing in the flow of information. And it is on this kind of clearly defined corner that a big laugh is hung.

THE VERY LAST WORD THEORY

Not only should your punchlines consist of as few words as possible, but ideally the complete idea of the punchline should not come into *full focus* until the very last word of the joke. That's one of the most natural ways to maximize the surprise. Also, if the meaning of your punchline becomes clear several words before the end of your sentence, when delivering the joke you're going to have to talk through the laugh. This almost always diminishes the laugh and should be avoided if at all possible. Preventing people from getting the joke until the very last word of the punchline also dramatically increases the odds of everyone in the audience getting the joke *at the exact same moment.* This too will maximize the laugh.

THE RULE OF NON-REPETITION

Whenever I'm working on a new joke, I try to keep in mind an idea I call the Rule of Non-Repetition. The rule is essentially this: Do not use any *key words* in the set-up that you plan to use in the punchline. In other words, don't repeat yourself. For example:

> *"I got one of those cycling helmets / you know,/ big white lump with the straps./ So of course I look like an idiot, right?/ Have to admit though, it is pretty comfortable./ So much so, I think I might get a* bike *to go with it."*

(Note that the slashes [/] appearing in the example indicate the points where, when delivering the joke, I pause for a beat or two to let the information register in the minds of the audience.)

When I first wrote this joke I considered using the words "bicycle helmet" in the set-up, but because I wanted to use the word "bike" in the punchline, I didn't want to repeat the *sound of the word.* That's just the kind of thing that can dull the teeth of a punchline. So I decided to use the word "cycling" instead, implying that I have a bike throughout the set-up, saving the word "bike" for the punchline.

BE SPECIFIC (BUT NOT TOO SPECIFIC)

When I deliver my jokes, I sometimes imagine I'm painting pictures in the minds of the audience.
—Steven Wright

When writing jokes, it's a good idea to avoid vague generalizations. Don't just talk about "fruit" when you can talk about "an apple." Strong writing creates a single image for everyone in the crowd, each person imagining a very similar thing. But when you say "fruit," people are either imagining several different kinds of fruit or they aren't really thinking of anything in particular, and both things can significantly reduce their emotional investment in the joke. But when you say "an apple," everyone has *a clear picture*, and thus a feeling.

But you can take this too far. If instead of "an apple" you say, "one of those red apples, with a slightly wilted stem and a couple of bruises near the bottom," chances are you have not only used far too many words, but also, instead of encouraging people to imagine an apple, by being overly specific you've probably frustrated some people's imaginations. Does the color and condition of the apple really matter to the joke? Ideally, your writing should be a clear, simple, and vivid invitation for people to imagine specific things and situations, rather than generalities. But you should try to avoid making your words so specific that they exclude too many people in your audience. It comes down to the idea of encouraging their imaginations, not limiting them.

IMMEDIATE VS. MEDIATED

I've seen shows where each of the comics had really strong sets, and a great variety of material was presented, but the biggest laugh of the night came from some comment made about a bald guy, or a heavy woman, sitting in the front row. This shouldn't come as a surprise. Not so much because the joke fulfilled the commonly held idea that comedy is about put-downs, but because the joke was about something *immediate*, something right there, right then. Like a prop gag, a joke about a person in the front row is about something shared by all present, something truly in the Here and Now. But the vast majority of the material stand-up comics write isn't about the Here and Now. Instead, it's about their dogs, childhoods, and trips to the bank. Mediated stuff that happened some other time, some other place. But there are ways to write material about things that happened at another place and time so that it expresses a more immediate sensibility.

IT HAPPENED TO YOU

Instead of telling jokes about stuff that happened to your friends, your neighbor, or even someone in the news, whenever possible write the joke so it's *about you*. After all, you're the one standing in front of the audience, so you're the one they are most likely to care about. And remember, if they don't care, they're not going to laugh. You are the audience's primary connection between your jokes and their interest, so do everything you can to make the jokes about you.

It Happened Yesterday

It's much easier for the audience to care about something that happened recently rather than six years ago. So just as you should try to write your jokes about you, try to write your jokes about stuff that "just happened." Remember, your task as a comic is to make the past live again, to speak of things that have already occurred, but somehow bring them kicking and screaming back into The Moment. That's tough enough without talking about stuff that happened ten years ago. Also, for the crowd to laugh at a joke, *it must be real for them*, and for it to be real for them it must first be real for you. You will have a much easier time making your jokes real for you if you're talking about stuff as if it happened just yesterday, the other day, or even last week.

Avoid Asking Questions

There are exceptions to every rule, but I believe it's a good idea to avoid writing jokes in the form of a question, like, "Have you ever noticed how . . . ?" or "Why is it whenever I go to the grocery store . . . ?" One or two in that vein are fine, and I've seen a number of comics do quite well with a handful of quick, funny questions, usually lumped together. But generally speaking I think questions should be avoided because, though often rhetorical, they sound like they are *asking the crowd for something*. And as I've already discussed, I think the comic should avoid seeming like he wants anything from the crowd (except perhaps that they listen to him). That way, the crowd feels free to relax, be themselves, and laugh.

AVOID LISTS

For some reason, many young comics write jokes in the form of lists, one set-up followed by a list of different punchlines:

> *"You know, folks, I figure there are only four different kinds of people that work at a fast food place . . ."*

Perhaps young comics have a tough time choosing between punchlines, so they decide to use them all. Or perhaps they simply have to work so darn hard to get the ideas they do, they can't bear not to use every one of them. I don't know. But I do know that, with the very rare exception, lists are to be avoided.

This is because when you begin to list stuff to a crowd, it immediately undercuts the idea that you are spontaneously speaking "off the top of your head." All of a sudden you're doing a routine, and that can really turn off a crowd. Also, when they realize you are doing a list, audiences no longer laugh at each punchline *like it's the last thing you're going to say on a topic*. You have explicitly let them know there's more to come, and knowing this, they will wait for it, holding back some of their laughter.

One way around this problem is to write a list in a more subtle fashion, so that it respects the idea of keeping the crowd unaware that there's more to come. Instead of using the phrase, "I figure it's either . . . or . . .," which signals to the crowd the fact that the joke has several parts, you could say, "I figure it's . . ." and say one of the punchlines. Then, after the laugh, say, "Or . . ." and deliver the second punchline. That way, they don't see the second punchline coming.

Though there are ways of effectively working with a joke with several punchlines, I believe it's usually a much better idea to commit to one, after experimenting with a few of your favorites. Perhaps you can rewrite one or two of the other punchlines to work as tags, but after that, I suggest you move on to another joke.

GESTURES REPLACING WORDS

The text is the actor's greatest enemy.
—Sanford Meisner

So much of the craft of stand-up is about economizing and editing—wringing the very most out of the very least. Of course, you should support what you say with your face and hands, bringing your words to life as much as possible. But sometimes, rather than merely reflecting something you say, a gesture can *replace* a word or even an entire sentence. For example, as part of a set-up you could say:

> *"I was walking down the street and I saw this sign for a restaurant that read, 'Rico's Pizzeria'. . . "*

But if you replace the five words, "for a restaurant that read" with the simple gesture of moving your right hand through the air as if it's pointing out the words on the sign, you can then say the set-up as:

> *"I was walking down the street and I saw this sign [hand gesture] 'Rico's Pizzeria'. . . "*

With one simple hand gesture, you've been able to drop five words from your set-up. In stand-up, that's a real communication victory.

THREE: THE MAGIC NUMBER

In almost every medium, in almost every culture, the number three seems to come up again and again. Three is fascinating because, while suggesting a balance (one in the middle and one on either side), it also suggests an instability, an "unfinishedness." It's a very vital number. One of the reasons the number three appears in so many

jokes is because comedy is all about breaking patterns—
but to break a pattern, one must first *establish a pattern.*
Something happening once doesn't establish a pattern, but
for it to happen twice, well that at least *suggests* a pattern.
And with the importance of extreme economy in comedy,
comics typically have something happen only twice
before breaking the suggested pattern with the third idea.

Breaking your information, especially dense punchlines,
into groups of three is also a very effective way to communicate. For example,

> *"It wasn't easy growing up as an only child./ I had to play*
> *lots of games by myself./ While other kids were playing*
> *catch/ I was playing* [1] *throw,/* [2] *walk,/ and* [3] *pick-*
> *up."*

In performance, the three-beat rhythm of the punchline plays a significant part in the joke's success.

SIMPLE IS BETTER

Never use a long word where a short one will do.
—George Orwell

Unlike you, the audience hasn't heard your jokes a thousand times. Every single word is new to them, and there's a
good chance they've been drinking. Also, when writing
material it's always a good idea to keep in mind the fact that
the people who make up the audiences in a comedy club
come from many different cultural, intellectual, and educational backgrounds.

Consequently, effective and trustworthy stand-up material is often simple and direct, without making too many intellectual or informational demands. Your jokes shouldn't require the audience to be filled with college graduates or pop-culture information junkies. However, writing material that has broad appeal and is expressed in clear and simple terms is very different from writing material that is dumb or uninspired. In fact, if you feel that you have to "talk down to the crowd," you are probably selling both yourself (and your audience!) short.

Almost every comic I've ever talked with has at some time felt disheartened by the *apparent* limitations of stand-up audiences. But despite my own difficult experiences, I still firmly believe this: Comedy club audiences consist of people with a wide range of life experiences, as well as dreams and disappointments and fears. And I too am a person with a wide range of life experiences, dreams, disappointments, and fears. As different as we may all be, we still have a great deal in common, and it is to the stuff we all have in common, our experiences as well as our imaginings, that the most successful stand-up material refers. Any limitations you perceive in your audience are more often an expression of *your own limitations* as a thinker and a communicator than anything else.

To me, the real challenge of writing stand-up is not to make my stuff as "dumb" as possible (anyone can do that!) but to express the abstract, imaginative, and unusual thoughts I have in terms that are as *simple and clear* as possible. Keep in mind, the act of simplification can be a sign of real intelligence and dedication. It's far easier to express strange and wonderful things in strange and wonderful terms. The inspired, imaginative, and even eloquent use of common, everyday language is a true challenge, worthy of any wordsmith. The eloquent use of simple words rather than the simple use of eloquent words. Speak your truth and speak it plainly. If a joke absolutely requires the use of big words or academic jargon, I urge you to consider dropping it. As someone once said, "If you have an idea and you can't write it down on a matchbook, it's probably not an important idea."

Excess Is Funny

Comedy is often about excess. Extremes are not only shocking and immensely engaging, they are also very clear. And stimulation and clarity are essential to stand-up. So when describing a situation or scenario, be as extreme as you can. Don't say, "I couldn't hear for close to an hour" when you can say, "I couldn't hear for *over* an hour." Push the limits, stretch things to the breaking point.

Editing

If it is possible to cut out a word, always cut it out.
—George Orwell

Aggressive editing is very important in joke writing in general, but particularly so when it comes to punchlines. If you take a few moments longer to blow up a balloon, no big deal. But every beat that passes between the moment you begin to pull the pin out of your pocket and the moment you actually burst the balloon is a beat that takes that tiny bit more of the edge off of the surprise.

Though an audience will be more forgiving of unnecessary words in a set-up than in a punchline, you still must be very strict on yourself when writing a set-up, especially given audiences expectations. To use the balloon analogy again, if you take a long time to blow up a really big balloon, when you burst it people expect a particularly loud bang. If, instead, the burst balloon mildly goes "pop," they're going to be disappointed. So remember, *the longer the set-up, the stronger the punchline must be.* In reference to a joke with an overly long set-up, Will Rogers once said, "That porch is too big for that house."

CALLBACKS

I find these fascinating. Basically, a comic makes a "callback" when he says a joke that *makes reference to information contained in a previous joke.* Most of the time, he's making a reference to one of his own jokes, something he said earlier in his set, but occasionally a comic will make a callback to a joke told by another comic earlier in the evening. Unlike most jokes, which derive their humor by making reference to experiences that the comic and the crowd share but that occurred outside of their relationship to each other, callbacks make reference to stuff that's been shared *since they met.* This explains why audiences often respond so positively to the experience of a callback. By "calling back" a fact the audience has in their heads, a fact that he himself gave them, the comic artfully completes a kind of psychological loop. At the same time, the comic is also playfully suggesting to the crowd, "Some of this stuff is scripted, folks!"

Incidently, you should keep in mind that the greater the amount of time elapsing between a callback and the information you're calling back to, the greater the chance of people not remembering, especially if they've been drinking. Personally, I try not to callback to anything more than ten minutes later. An exception to this is if I'm doing a repeated callback, referring back to a fact *several times* in a set. In such a case, after you've done it two or three times, I think it's safe to let as much as thirty minutes go by and still make another callback.

Writing with Other People

Start with, "I think it's a masterpiece!" then tell me what you think could be changed.

—Tim Robbins

One of the keys to comics writing well together, apart from liking each other and respecting each other's work, is for both comics to have a clear idea of the other comic's *character and perspective.* If they don't quite know where the other is coming from, they are going to be forever suggesting stuff that simply doesn't suit that person's character. Another good idea is for both comics to encourage a very positive, supportive energy. Saying, "I don't think that's funny" can often be the kiss of death for a young, creative relationship.

Instead, you might want to try a numerical system. Suggest an idea, and ask the other comic to tell you what he thinks a crowd's reaction to it might be, based on a scale from one to five. I think it's very important (not to mention humble) for both comics to emphasize that they are only ever giving their personal "two cents," guesses really. The audience has the only vote that counts, and until the bit is tried onstage, you just never know.

S A N K E Y

PAVAROTTI AND FRIENDS

WHY KEEP WRITING?

Originality and the feeling of one's dignity are achieved only through work and struggle.

—Dostoyevsky

You have an hour of strong, tried-and-true material. Why write any more jokes? Many comics get tired of doing the same material again and again, and as they get tired, so do their performances. Having a constant flow of new material, even just a few new jokes, can keep things fresh and interesting, if only for you. Also, you may all of a sudden start touring more, maybe even getting to some cities several times a year, and that's when it's really important to have some new material. The last thing you want is for people who "enjoyed you so much the last time" to come out to see you again, only to find that you're doing all the same stuff. Club owners also get tired of seeing the same material, and though, strictly speaking, they aren't really your audience, they are decision makers on whom you want to make a good impression. A new joke they particularly like can go a long way toward making you memorable. As you continue to write, you'll find you start creating different kinds of material. The jokes comics write in their fourth years are often very different from the jokes they write in their tenth years.

JOKES ARE VEHICLES

The practice of Zen is forgetting the self in the act of uniting with something.

—Koun Yamada

A funny, well-written joke is a thing of beauty. A small wonder. But even a great joke is not an end in itself. Instead, I believe a joke's true power lies in its use as a vehicle of expression for the comic, and as a vehicle for connection with an audience. A fine joke, and the laughs it yields, can also be an amazing vehicle of release and ultimately of enlightenment. Jokes, after all, are vehicles for sharing.

JOKE CHECKLIST

1. Is the joke about something most people care about?
2. How do you feel about what you are saying?
3. Is the joke credible?
4. Is there a definite "click moment"?
5. Have you planned your emphases and pauses to highlight key information?
6. Can you remove any words from the set-up or punchline?
7. Can you replace any words with a gesture?
8. Are you really bringing the joke to life with your face, hands, and body?

CHAPTER THREE

CHARACTER

Your stage character is the magic glue. It makes sense of all your jokes, giving them a context to spring out of and a perspective to reflect. If your material is the *what*, then your delivery the *how*, your timing the *when*, and your character the *who*.

Your character also keeps you in touch with your material and with your audience. To borrow a distinction from Marshall McLuhan, if your jokes are the message, your character is the medium. Then again, one could just as fairly say your character is the message, and your jokes are the medium. I don't mean to be confusing, it's just that, ideally, a comic's character and his material should clearly *express each other*. In a sense, character and material are really just different ways of looking at the same thing. Namely, the comic's performance itself.

WHAT'S THE DIFFERENCE BETWEEN A COMIC AND AN ACTOR?

Stand-up comedy is a particular kind of popular theater. It's very similar to traditional acting in that there is a script, and the actor must remember his lines and deliver them with conviction. But the emotional range of a typical stand-up comedy show, both as explored by the comic and experienced by the audience, is much more limited than that of a traditional play. Plays often touch on everything from love and fear to sorrow and vengeance. Stand-up is almost strictly about getting laughs. Yes, a comic may well deal with very significant, even profound issues, but in the end, no matter what the comic's personal aspirations, people go to a comedy club to drink and to laugh—even though many of the best stand-ups are quite good actors, delivering their material with inspired energy and a strong sense of stagecraft.

Many of the differences between traditional theater and contemporary stand-up lie, not merely in the performing style, but in the very different *performance situations*. Theater audiences are sober and sit in relative silence, while comedy club audiences drink, smoke, order food, and sometimes even chat during shows. Theater audiences often pay a fair bit more for a ticket than comedy-club goers. And though comedy-club shows and plays are both usually around two hours in length, at the theater one expects to see several people performing together, while at clubs the audience expects to see several people performing individually. These very different working conditions cannot help but dramatically influence the craft and attitudes of the actors themselves.

Another significant difference between stand-ups and traditional actors is that people don't really think of stand-ups *as actors*. Though stage actors certainly strive for a freshness and apparent spontaneity in their performances, audiences are fully aware that there is a script they must closely follow, often to the word. But stand-up comics, as unspontaneous as they often truly are, are generally considered to be much more spontaneous creatures than actors. In fact, it's this belief in the "extemporaneous sharing of stand-up comics" that is one of stand-up's most powerful myths.

Many professional comics alter their sets on a regular basis and often make comments off the tops of their heads, but the great majority of what comes out of their mouths is very tightly scripted indeed. In reality, stand-up comics are nothing more than actors, *playing the part of stand-up comics*.

MAGNIFYING GLASS OR TELESCOPE?

Most comics are magnifying glasses, far fewer are telescopes. One of the most popular styles of contemporary stand-up is that of "observational humor." The comic takes an everyday experience, something most people can relate to (e.g., a joke about going to the laundromat) and with his insight finds the humor in it. The comic is a magnifying glass, looking closely at the things of our immediate lives and telling us what he sees. But as popular and common as this approach to stand-up is, it is still nonetheless only one approach.

Another style, adopted far less often than that of the magnifying glass, is the telescope style. With this approach, the comic's jokes are based not on our collective experiences of this world, but on the comic's individual experiences of another world, namely his imagination (e.g., a joke about being married to a kangaroo). These comics share with their audiences descriptions of a place where their audiences do not live (despite any parallels that may exist to their own world), and in this way the comic acts like a telescope, bringing a strange, faraway place into focus.

Of course, both approaches require craft and dedication, but I believe that the magnifying glass approach is easier to sell to a North American crowd than the telescope approach. As a magnifying glass, the comic's material deals directly with the audience's own life experiences, appealing to their own egocentric, self-absorbed natures. The comic's material also explores his own immediate life experiences, so it is easier for him to deliver the material and bring it to life.

In contrast, the magnifying glass approach requires the audience to *use their imaginations*, rather than just their memories, as the comic speaks of things they've never seen with their own eyes. This approach also requires the comic himself to do more than simply rely on his direct life experiences, demanding that he stretch his own imagination to the fullest.

Both approaches have their beauty. As a magnifying glass, the comic makes us more aware of the humor in the world around us. And by almost magically revealing to us the extent to which our personal experiences are in fact *shared*, he brings us closer together. And as a telescope, the comic challenges our imaginations, asking us to both think and feel about not how things are, but how they *could be*.

WHY NOT JUST BE YOURSELF?

Characters are interesting if they passionately believe in what they're talking about.

—Martin Short

I've heard many experienced comics say to beginners "Just be yourself." Ultimately, I believe this is pretty good advice, but I also think telling that to a young performer is a lot like telling a young driver, "Just don't hit any of the other cars." Not so much because it's obvious, but because it's not particularly instructive or helpful. A young performer may not be completely clear on *who exactly he is.* Knowing who you are is no easy feat, let alone knowing how to bring that to the stage.

By all means, try to focus on your own unique sense of humor rather than on trying to deliver material that doesn't suit the person you really are. But being funny *offstage* and being funny *onstage* are very, very different kinds of "funny." The most successful comics tend to play characters that are two things: real and exaggerated. It's almost a paradox, but not quite. Imagine, if you will, a pie cut into eight pieces, and let's say that each piece of the pie represents one of the dominant characteristics of who you really are (anxious, cerebral, shy, loud, etc.). Now, what successful stand-ups tend to do is to *concentrate* on one or two of the pieces of their pie, and then exaggerate the degree to which these real characteristics dominate their personality. That way, they get to draw energy from real-life characteristics, but they also present a character who is inherently theatrical and powerful onstage.

INNER CHILD

Think of it this way. To "play a part" is really to "display a part." A part of who? Yourself. Many film actors say that they can only do justice to a character in a movie if they feel they can strongly relate to the role. Being able to relate to something is another way of saying that there is a commonality between you and the thing you are relating to.

So be yourself onstage, but be your likable, vulnerable, unique, engaging, interesting, powerful, and above all else FUNNY self.

LIKABILITY AND VULNERABILITY

Zen is to have the heart and soul of a little child.

—Takuan

There are many things to consider when it comes to your stage character, but without a doubt the two most important qualities you should strive to obtain are Likability and Vulnerability. If you can achieve these two the majority of the times you take the stage, you will be well on your way to being a successful stand-up comic. You cannot overestimate their importance.

There's an old show biz expression, "If they like you, you can do no wrong. And if they don't like you . . . good luck." In my experience, this is completely, almost frighteningly true. Nothing is more powerful than the crowd's liking you. They will give you more room for error, more time before they get bored, and they will laugh harder when you're funny. Liking you, the audience is simply more receptive, more patient, and more responsive. But if you've said or done something to make the crowd take a disliking to you, especially early in your set . . . good luck. It's amazing how quickly a crowd can cool to a performer.

How can you maximize likability? You can start by respecting your audience and caring about what they think and feel. Crowds sense if you care about them. And yes, sometimes the crowd likes it when a comic "ruffles their hair" by pretending not to care about their opinion, not unlike when lovers play at being tough with each other. But if the crowd suspects you aren't feigning your disregard, they will turn on you.

Another thing you can do to be likable is *smile*. I know

it sounds obvious, but go to a stand-up show and watch, just watch, how many comics fail to smile a lot onstage. If you have to force a smile, forget it. Crowds are also very sensitive to insincerity, so if you are actually more comfortable frowning, frown. Then again, if you can't sincerely greet an audience of people who have paid to watch you with a smile, you may want to consider another line of work.

Audiences tend to give respect and power to those performers who, in turn, grant them respect and power. This is where *vulnerability* comes in. Audiences need to believe they are having a definite influence on the comic. That they aren't just another crowd. But for them to believe they can influence you, you must first seem open to them—or even better you must in some way seem to be a little bit *fragile*. However subtle, an air of vulnerability brings with it a sense of being both honest and sensitive, qualities that can greatly enhance a performer's image in the eyes of the audience. When a performer meets an audience, it's a little bit like a seduction. Ultimately, he can only take a crowd *where they are willing to go*.

INTELLIGENCE

It's the less intelligent comics that tend to try to come off as very smart, and the more intelligent comics that tend to play down their intellect.

—Woody Allen

If comedic wit isn't literally the same thing as intelligence, it's certainly often a strong indication of intelligence. Perhaps it's because of this that audiences often expect a comic to be "smart" or "clever" as well as funny. But as always, there are ways of displaying your intelligence onstage that will *work for you*, and ways that will *work against you*.

Whenever considering a new approach or attitude to your performance, always first ask yourself not "Will this be funny?" but "Will this bring the audience and me closer?" The audience will always tell you with their laughter or their silence what is and isn't funny, but *developing trust* with them is a much more subtle thing.

That's what makes the display of intelligence onstage so intriguing. Crowds will admire you if you can give them a flash of your smarts without coming off as somehow superior to them. But if, for even an instant, they suspect you think you are intellectually "above them," they will quickly cool to you, perhaps even become hostile. The comic "pulling attitude" onstage is exactly the kind of thing that literally *creates* hecklers.

So by all means, cultivate an active intelligence in your work, but try not to be too bold about it or take too much obvious pleasure from it. Humility, even if it's only apparent, will always serve you well onstage. To my mind, I think it requires more real intelligence to display your smarts in an indirect and imaginative fashion than in an obvious, "Look how clever I am" fashion. It also tends to be much more interesting to watch.

VITALITY

An ounce of behavior is worth a pound of words.
—Sanford Meisner

Stand-up is about energy. The energy you *give to* the crowd, and the energy you *receive from* the crowd. The meaning of the words you speak are important, but they are also important as bearers of energy. In this regard, your *actions* onstage, how you stand and move, are of even greater importance.

Not surprisingly, the more fully and richly your actions onstage reflect a *definite* character, the more engaging, memorable, and believable the character will be. People respond to the living, especially to what speaks to them and their own lives. In fact, art theorists often suggest that the more vital and alive a work of art is, the more apt people are to respond to it. At all times your goal should be to fill your character with real energy, ideally rendering him or her "larger than life."

NOVELTY

Unfortunately, the word "novelty" has a negative, belittling association. When people refer to something as a novelty they usually mean that it is somehow new or interesting, but also that it is of little importance or consequence. I think that's too bad. Perhaps novelty merely for novelty's sake, without any substance or insight, is to be avoided. But if, among many other qualities, your stage character also happens to be novel, all the better.

When it comes to your stage character (or almost anything for that matter) you can approach things in one of four ways. You can do something:

1. old in an old way
2. old in a new way
3. new in an old way
4. new in a new way.

Take singing a song, for example. You can sing an old song in an old way. This may strike people as quite unoriginal and, frankly, rather dull. Or you can sing an old song in a new way. It being an old song, people will be able to relate to it, and perhaps even enjoy its familiarity, but because of the new way you sing it, they will also find it interesting and stimulating. Or you can sing a new song in an old way. This combination will again have an aspect people can relate to, namely the old way you sing it, but being a new song, it will also be interesting. Or, finally, you can sing a new song in a new way. This approach is both the most challenging and, from a communications perspective, the most risky. With both a new song and a new way of singing, people may well find it intriguing, but will also have nothing familiar to hold on to. Often, if people find something too challenging, they simply won't bother trying to understand it. And although what you do may be wonderful, perhaps even ingenious, if people aren't listening, you have failed to communicate.

It's in an attempt to be novel that many comics search for a "hook," something about their look or character or perspective that is both unique and commercial. But more often than not it is not something that can be forced into existence. Instead, truly effective hooks, with staying power and credibility, tend to naturally grow out of a character and act developed over many years.

DISTINCTIVENESS VS. BROAD APPEAL

We live to survive our paradoxes.
—The Tragically Hip

This is the classic artist/marketing dilemma. Two diametrically opposed views that are each so important and fundamental, they are capable of pulling a comic apart at the seams. And however you decide on this issue, it can't help but have dramatic impact on literally every aspect of your work. Your character, your delivery, your material, everything.

Here's the problem: The more unusual and atypical your approach to stand-up, the more memorable and distinctive you will be. But . . . the more distinctive you are, the more *limited* your appeal might well be, the less accessible your act is, and the more doors will be closed to you. For example, if you always went onstage nude, Lord knows you would be remembered, but I suspect you would also be locked up. Your only market would be nudist colonies. Distinctive, but of limited appeal.

But if, in an attempt to go for the broadest appeal possible, you take a very conventional and typical approach to stand-up, you might end up as a completely unoriginal and utterly forgettable performer. I'm sorry to say I have no idea what the solution to this dilemma is, but I definitely think you should keep it in mind and try to arrive at your own answers.

PERSPECTIVE

Simply put, a perspective is *the way someone sees something*. In this case, the "someone" is your stage character, and the "something" is the world around him or her. What's your character's take on politics? Food? What's his favorite movie? To arrive at the answers to these relatively specific questions, you should probably first ask broader questions. Is your character really smart or a little dumb? Is he optimistic or pessimistic? Well spoken or crass? The more you know about your character, the more fully he'll come to life onstage, even if you don't actually make a point of relaying this information to the audience through your jokes. Having a clearly defined idea of exactly who your character is will go a long way toward the creation of a consistent perspective. And consistency is essential if your character is going to remain credible throughout your entire set.

FACTS AND FEELINGS

We should take care not to make the intellect our god; it has, of course, powerful muscles, but no personality.
—Albert Einstein

One part of your character's consistency is the *factual* information contained in your material. If you tell a joke about a woman you've been dating for a few months, and then a minute later tell a joke about not having had a girlfriend for years, you're going to put the crowd's belief in jeopardy. Your jokes must fit together and reflect a single reality.

But an even more important aspect of this idea of consistency is that of your character's *emotional responses* to a range of subjects. If he seems insecure and shy about women one moment, and then casual and confident the next, this can subtly undermine your character's credibility. Being aware of the factual information you give to an audience will be much easier to monitor than the emotional information, but I believe it is the emotional world of your character that will set the tone of your set far more than the details of your jokes.

KEY WORDS AND CATCH PHRASES

"No respect!"

—Rodney Dangerfield

In two simple words, Dangerfield has a touchstone for his character. A phrase both he and the crowd can focus on and, in a sense, experience his comedy *through*. Whether or not you go so far as to actually say a catch phrase onstage (a few words you say again and again throughout your set), it's a good idea to at least have a few key words to focus on, especially just before going onstage when you want to "get into character." So think about some words that might lie at the core of your character onstage, and perhaps even what you want to be known for. Thinking of some comics I've seen, words like intense, babbling, menacing, jovial, depressed, emotional—all come to mind. Find the words that best reflect the idea and feeling of your character, and then follow them like guiding lights in the fog.

CHARACTER-DRIVEN MATERIAL

There are many jokes that almost anyone can tell and get a laugh with. Usually, that's because the jokes are: (1) simple, and (2) refer to things that are common knowledge. Jokes like this are fine. In fact, they are often the most trustworthy of jokes. But they are different from character-driven material, material that virtually *requires the audience to view the performer in a specific light.* For example, Milton Berle became famous for wearing a dress onstage. It became part of his stage character. In his day, if another comic wore a dress onstage, the crowd either didn't know what to make of it or they thought that the comic was "doing Milton Berle's bit."

Once you get a clear idea of your stage character, so much of the craft of stand-up is made that much easier. Ideally, your jokes, your "look," even your promotional material should be reflections of your character and of your comedic perspective. And as your character comes into focus for you, you'll find yourself writing material specifically for that character. Think of that character as a picture frame and everything you do and say onstage as the picture. The character defines, frames, and literally "makes sense" of your material, especially in the minds of the audience.

Imagine if you will that during the first few minutes of your set, the material you deliver lets the audience know how the world looks through the eyes of your character. That's why you should think of the material you choose for your first few minutes as "defining." After that, the audience almost takes on that perspective, that sensibility, and becomes more comfortable with that outlook on the world as your set progresses.

On one hand this can be a little restrictive because, after doing five minutes of jokes about how much you love kids, the audience may not know how to respond if you then want to do a joke about using children as slave labor in a butterscotch pudding factory. They've become accustomed to seeing you in a certain light, and may resist change. On the other hand, now that they've come to know your character a little better, you can really start to explore, and have fun with, that very character.

The Stealability Test

Here's a thought. "The degree to which other comics can use your material, and still have good success with it, is the degree to which your material is impersonal and unoriginal." Think about that for a moment. Certainly, almost every comic you will ever see will have jokes that many other comics could do well with. In fact, that is often the sign of a good joke. But, more often than not, the jokes a comic *becomes famous for* are jokes that only he or she can get away with. That's because they are jokes that either really only suit his or her stage character or because that stage character is particularly well-suited to delivering those jokes. Many famous comics do bits that, done by another comic, would come off as unnatural or even just plain dumb. That's one of the magical qualities of character-driven comedy.

SIMPLE AND CLEAR

Don't do anything unless something happens to make you do it.
—Sanford Meisner

There's an old story about a man going into a store to buy a ladle. There were many to choose from, but in the end he narrowed it down to three ladles. Two of them featured lovely, intricate patterns on their handles and bowls, while the third ladle was completely unadorned, almost plain. Then, when the man asked about the price of the ladles, he was shocked to hear that the plain ladle was almost double the price of the other two. But the salesman explained to him, "You see, the unadorned ladle is of a much higher quality and must be of absolutely perfect workmanship because, unlike the other ones with intricate patterns, on the simple ladle there is no place to hide the flaws."

When developing your stage character—or working on any aspect of stand-up, for that matter—it's *very* easy to make things more complicated than they need to be. It's keeping things simple that's truly difficult. But we are all where we are at, no place else, and beginners in almost all crafts and disciplines tend to overcomplicate things. Between their young egos and vast ignorance, labored complications act almost like a buffer, as they, being beginners, trip and stumble and fall time and again. But if you read the writings of acknowledged masters of many disciplines, the idea of simplicity comes up more often than not.

Simple isn't easy, and keeping things simple and clear is a *very different* thing from keeping things stupid or superficial. It usually takes great intelligence and a lot of hard work to simplify anything. To cut out the extraneous, clear away the incidental. But if you keep working at it, it can be done. Just keep asking yourself, why am I doing this? Is it meaningful? Is it needed? What does it serve? Remember, if in doubt, cut it out.

COMMITMENT

Put your heart, mind, intellect, and soul even to your smallest acts. This is the secret to success.
—Swami Sivananda

As Shakespeare wrote, "half measures avail us nothing." This is particularly so in comedy. You will only succeed with your character and material to the degree to which you commit to it. It's really that simple. Do what you do with *less than all of you*, and that is exactly what the audience will give back. Actually, the idea of commitment is so important, I've often thought that it's not so much what a performer does onstage, or even how a performer does what he does onstage, but *how much of himself he puts into it*. Go to a few stand-up shows, see how the comics who really give their all almost always do better than the comics who don't. Material is very important, make no mistake about it. But commitment is just as important. Onstage, stay focused on your character. Don't be thinking about something else. And try not to worry or be afraid. Fearlessly give of yourself, through your character, to the audience. Commit. Be *there* for them, and more often than not, they will be there for you.

CLOTHING

A few years ago, I was talking with an amateur comic just before he went onstage, and he was telling me how he felt his clothes effectively supported his character onstage. He then asked me what I thought of his shoes, and I said, "If they notice your shoes, you aren't funny." I still think there's a lot of truth in what I rather ungently said, especially when you consider that 95 percent of the crowd is only ever going to see you from the waist up. But I also very much agree with Canadian comic Ronnie Edwards, who once told me, "The outside *must* reflect the inside."

In the same way that intro music can set a tone or communicate a subtle message, your clothes can tell the crowd a great deal. Steve Martin used to always wear a white suit, and Sam Kinison often wore a trench coat and an oversized beret. Now, for just a moment, try to imagine Steve Martin in the overcoat or Kinison in the white suit. See what I mean? Clothes really say *a lot.* And, like it or not, your clothes are going to express something, so it's up to you to decide whether they are going to work "with you" or "against you."

As always, the answers to your questions concerning what to wear onstage will be found by referring to your ideas about your stage character. Who is he? What's he like? What kinds of things does he talk about onstage? Is he tidy? Unkempt? Casual? Sensual? Sometimes, waiting to board a train or plane, I'll make a point of flipping through some fashion magazines, keeping my stage character in mind, just to see if I come across some clothes that I'd like to try onstage.

SHOES

As I've already mentioned, I think the shoes you wear are pretty much a non-issue, given the audience's sight lines, but they should be very comfortable. I usually wear running shoes.

PANTS

Again, they should be comfortable, but they should also reflect your character's sensibilities. Baggy pants? Jeans? Expensive-looking dress pants? If I'm only doing a short spot on a show I often wear blue jeans, but if I'm headlining I tend to avoid blue jeans, going with black jeans or casual dress pants.

SUITS AND TIES

I never wear a suit and tie onstage. Never. I don't feel comfortable, I get way too hot, and I don't believe it suits my character. But a lot of comics seem to think, "If I'm headlining, I better wear a tie," which, to my mind, is a bit silly. Fine if a tie goes with your character, but if it really doesn't go with your character I would avoid it. A nice suit and tie can send signals of success and professionalism to certain crowds, but it also has an air of "establishment" about it that can work against you, particularly with younger crowds. Then again, perhaps there's something to be said for the old stand-up adage, "Dress like a headliner, become a headliner."

SHIRTS

This is the one piece of your wardrobe the crowd will be looking at through your entire set, and I think it's something you should spend some time thinking about. With or without a collar? Sleeves rolled up or down? And, of course, what color or pattern? Every detail sends different messages to the crowd, particularly in our clothes-conscious culture.

As a rule of thumb, I wear lighter-colored shirts at bar gigs and "one-nighters" because they tend to have poor lighting and I want to make sure my face and body really "pull the eyes" from across the room. I want to be very watchable. In club gigs I always try to wear a shirt that is a simple contrast to whatever wall is behind me. And if I don't know the room beforehand, I'll often bring two shirts so I have a choice. I tend to avoid shirts with really crazy, bright colors or patterns, as well as shirts with pictures or large logos because I don't want them to pull focus from my face.

WOMEN'S CLOTHING

Having never worn traditional women's clothing onstage, I don't have much to say on this subject, except, perhaps, if you are a man and you want to wear a dress onstage, be prepared for the audience to not be quite sure what to make of you (despite Milton Berle). And if you are a woman, well, my heart goes out to you because, based on my limited understanding, women have a more complicated time dressing for the stage.

You'd think it would never hurt to look your best, but I know women comics who deliberately *play down* their attractiveness, saying it can make women in the crowd jealous and distract men from focusing on their *minds* rather than their physical selves. Then again, I've had women comics tell me that if they wear clothing that is too androgynous, people think they are lesbians, and (as silly as it sounds) that too can be distracting. It's interesting, but there *does* seem to be a conspicuous lack of typically "beautiful" women making it big in stand-up comedy. Maybe that's because they get wooed away to television and movies. I don't know.

SUNGLASSES

These can look very interesting onstage. Mysterious, funky, sexy, lots of things. But they also cover your eyes. Not only can this come off looking guarded, but it also blocks one of your most powerful means of staying connected with a crowd. Besides, wearing sunglasses in a comedy club can look quite staged and unnatural. So if you want to experiment with sunglasses, realize you do so at a great risk.

CLOTHING CHECKLIST

All in all, when it comes to the question of clothing, there are five factors to take into account, each of which I believe is quite important.

COMFORT
Do your clothes make you feel too hot? Too cool? Are they too tight or too loose? Do you feel "right" in them, or do you feel awkward? To be the best performer you

can be, feeling comfortable and relaxed is absolutely essential. Anything that limits that should be questioned.

FUNCTION

Do you have pockets for anything you may need? Do your clothes make you stand out from the back wall of the stage, or do they make your body blend in and vanish? Do your clothes wrinkle or show their wear and tear too easily (not good for life on the road)? Also, where is the gig? A meeting room in a fine hotel? A biker bar? Like a lot of other comics, I often dress more casually, sometimes even a little bit tougher, if I'm working a particularly gritty room. With your clothing, as with all aspects of the craft of stand-up, always take your audience into account.

CHARACTER

Are your clothes credible? Are they something your character would wear? Looking at your clothes, do they reflect the handful of words that best describe your character, or do your clothes look forced and unnatural?

ATTRACTIVENESS

Do you look decidedly unattractive in your clothes? This is a strange one; after all, stand-up is about ideas, feelings, imagination, and acting, not looking good, right? Yes . . . but it can't hurt if you also happen to look your best. This is one issue I personally do not take as seriously as some of the others. If I know certain clothes look really good on me, but they don't suit my character, I simply won't wear them. Instead, I'll look for a compromise, something that looks OK on me but is also the kind of thing my character might wear.

And speaking of looking good, I've heard more than a few comics say, "The nicer you dress, the dirtier your material can be." And again, I suspect there's some truth to this. I've often seen a crowd groan at a comic wearing a jean jacket delivering slightly off-color stuff, and then twenty minutes later freely laugh at a comic in a suit and tie delivering much rougher material. Mind you, I can't say being able to get away with being as dirty as possible is one of my personal goals, but this does, once again, attest to the power of clothing.

DISTINCTIVENESS

This is another tricky issue, one I definitely compromise on. I remember reading a book by Richard Belzer in which he referred to comics who deliberately dress bizarrely as "my-look-is-my-act" comics. I'm still undecided on this issue. If what you're wearing comes across to the crowd as fake, forced, or "trying too hard," it's probably not going to work. On the other hand, *if it suits your character* (to walk onstage in a blood-soaked apron) and it also happens to be something that makes you stand out and be memorable to a crowd, well, that's a good thing, isn't it?

CHAPTER FOUR

DELIVERY

Fine art is that in which the hand, the head, and the heart go together.
—Ruskin, *The Two Paths*

To put it simply, a comic's delivery is *how* he says what he says. Not just with his voice, but also with his face, hands, and body. And it's not just about what he says and does, but also about what he *doesn't* say or do. Does he start a particular sentence with his voice slightly raised and then lower the timbre of his voice as he nears the end of the sentence? Does he plant a large, pregnant pause just before the last word? Does he say the line more like a question than a statement? Does he whisper it? Shout it? Does his voice sound like that of an educated, academic person or like someone more down-to-earth?

As unique and personal as a comic's jokes can be, a comic's delivery is more personal still. Delivery is also a very subtle thing, much more difficult to analyze and discuss than the words that make up a particular joke.

SHOULD YOU USE YOUR REAL VOICE?

Many comics insist that you should deliver your material in your own, "real" speaking voice. But I must confess, I am often suspicious of whatever I hear many comics stating as dogma. I do agree that you will probably have more success with a voice that doesn't sound like you're trying too hard, but I also can't imagine, offstage, Sam Kinison only ever shouted. Or that Bobcat Goldthwait always sounds so bizarre. Or even that the "real" Steven Wright never gets even a little bit animated when talking. Once again, there are no rules without exceptions. And remember, it's the exceptional comics who tend to make it big. Then again, it's the comics who refuse to acknowledge certain fundamentals who bomb time and again.

EXPERIMENT

A few years ago I had a cold so bad ("How bad was it?") that, normally, I would not have performed a show. But for some reason or other I decided to take a gig anyway. I probably needed the money. When I crawled to the stage I felt so weak, feverish, and congested, it was all I could do to stand up there and recite my jokes in a quiet, monotonous voice. I had no energy to really "sell" the jokes, and though I am usually a very physical, animated performer and I really modulate my voice, on this occasion I was as still as a mannequin and I delivered my material in a decidedly flat fashion.

Surprisingly, I did quite well. I didn't kill, but I was fascinated by the fact that so much of what I usually put into the delivery of my material was missing, *yet the crowd still enjoyed themselves*. Perhaps it says something about the strength of the material, perhaps it says something about the efficacy of such a relaxed delivery. Who knows? But it was a real reminder to me to continue to stay open to different deliveries. Play with your voice, *experiment*. Deliver your material in a variety of different tempos and pitches, putting emphases on different words. It's a great way to discover what works best for you, while also learning about your capabilities.

VARIETY VS. A UNIFORM STYLE

The longer the set, the greater the chances of the audience getting bored with a particular style of delivery. Not just the sound of the comic's voice, but also his tempo or rhythm. I've seen many comics who do well in a ten-minute set have a very mediocre thirty- or forty-minute set because the crowd grew tired of them. These comics lack the range to hold a crowd's attention, and developing a powerful delivery can be an important part of holding people's attention.

For example, let's say a comic only ever whispered. Now, I think this could make for a very engaging style . . . for about five minutes. Although it *would* be unique and memorable. On the other hand, a comic could develop a pleasing, simple speaking style that had a lot of range to it, a voice that easily carried different emotions, from anger to ecstasy, and one that a crowd could happily listen to for over an hour. But two weeks later, which delivery would the crowd be more likely to remember? I fear it would be the comic who only ever whispered. So here again is that recurring question of something unique and memorable versus something more natural and accessible, but perhaps also more forgettable.

Whatever style you eventually adopt, when delivering your material strive to *stay interesting*. Continue to fuel the crowd's curiousity. As always, the key is stimulation. The more stimulating your delivery, the more it will engage the audience, and the more they will really be there with you.

PROJECTION AND EMOTION

One of the many things that sets experienced comics apart from beginners is the degree to which these seasoned comics magnify, clarify, and commit to their material. When speaking to a friend on the phone, we all try to be relatively clear and engaging. But, as actors are fond of saying, "Onstage, everything must be larger." In a word, exaggerated.

With this in mind, even if you decide to use your "real" voice onstage (hopefully after some experimentation!), it's probably not a good idea to deliver your jokes *exactly* as you say everything else in your day. For starters, depending on the mike, you may have to project your voice a little more than usual in order for the people at the back to hear you above the pinball machines. Also, while your friends (people who know you very well) will be able to read the subtle signs in your voice to determine how you feel about what you're saying, the 300 intoxicated strangers in front of the stage are going to require you to convey your feelings in a clearer fashion. This often involves exaggerating the pleasure or anger or whatever in the sound of your voice—in other words, acting.

I fully realize that to you this may seem very obvious, but I've watched many comics onstage who don't seem particularly interested in being clearly understood apart from the *meaning* of the words they use. And yet, when it comes to stand-up, *how* you deliver your words is *at least as important* as their meaning. So much so that, if I wanted to communicate to an audience the idea that I am angry, and I had to choose between saying, "I am angry" in a quiet, flat, tone or shouting "Hampsters and horseshoes!" in a very loud, furious, expressive voice, I would definitely deliver the latter.

How Do You Feel About What You Are Saying?

The truth of a thing is the feel of it, not the think of it.
—Stanley Kubrick

This is crucial. Are you happy about what you're talking about? Sad? Puzzled? Aroused? Unless you are clear about how you feel, how can the crowd be? And if they are not clear about something, anything, it can only lessen the degree to which they will respond to what you are saying. This is especially so when you are saying something provocative. For example, if you are talking about necrophilia (sex with the very, very sleepy) many in the crowd will need to have a sense of how you feel about what you're saying *before* they'll feel comfortable to laugh—"Does he think necrophilia is fine and dandy?" How you deliver your words can be a big help in conveying this. Remember, just as comics tend to speak too quickly more often than too slowly, comics also tend to *under*emphasize their feelings onstage more often than *over*emphasize. Don't be afraid to show how you feel! Remember, if the joke is the sail, your feelings are the wind.

And even more generally, whenever you deliver your material, it should be clear to the crowd that, however you happen to feel about what you are saying, you always *care strongly* about it, that what you are talking about is important to you. This is crucial, because if *you* don't seem to care about what you are saying . . . why should the audience? A crowd will only invest as much in your words as you do. I've said it before (and I'm sure I'll say it again) you only get as much *out* of an experience as you're willing to put *into* it. This is especially true onstage.

EVERY SENTENCE YOUR LAST

Considering that *surprise* is such an important part of effective comedy, one subtle means of maintaining this tension in a crowd, this giddying sense of being off-balance, is to deliver each line as if it's your last (at least on that particular subject). Try to forget that you have several more tags to the punchline.

This is effective in two ways. *First,* in thinking that the comic has no more little quips or lines coming, that he is done for now, the crowd will feel free to completely release whatever tension/laughter has built up inside them, instead of holding a bit in for the next line. This results in a bigger, louder laugh. And *second,* it sets up the audience for a tiny surprise when you have yet another tag for the punchline. This again, yields a bigger laugh. I don't believe the crowd consciously thinks about holding back laughter or about whether the comic has another line coming, but I certainly do believe that some form of unconscious regulating *is* occurring. The content of the tag offers *explicit* surprise, and the mere existence of the tag offers *implicit* surprise. More surprise, more laughter.

If asked, many comedy-club goers would probably say they believe that a fair bit of what comics say is in fact scripted, yet the illusion most comics strive for is that it's all just coming off the top of their heads. Delivering your lines in an extemporaneous fashion, as if each is the last, goes a long way toward supporting this fundamental illusion.

STEPPING ON THE LAUGH

Sometimes, a steady, unbroken rhythm of joke, laugh, joke, laugh, joke, laugh, can be very effective, but sometimes comics want to break that rhythm—to give the crowd a chance to catch their breath, to maximize modulation and variety, for stimulation's sake, for a lot of reasons. One of the ways to do this is to step on the laugh. Rather than delivering a line and giving the crowd a chance to fully express the laugh, you deliver a line, and then begin delivering the next line *before they've completely finished laughing at the previous one.* Their laughter has not been given full release, so the dregs of it are still in their chests. This can be dangerous because they can grow frustrated and even tired, but if it is done quickly, with a number of short lines in a row, and *then* you deliver one last line on the subject, it can often yield an applause break. Which, frankly, is always nice.

PAUSING AND EMPHASIZING

Logical pauses serve our brains, psychological pauses serve our feelings.

—Stanislavski

I really enjoy pausing between jokes, between words, even between syllables. During a pause, a comic *can* lose the crowd's focus or appear to be trying to think of a joke (never a good thing), but pausing can be a wonderful way to *create curiosity*, give the crowd a chance to catch their breath, and *build tension* that is then burst with a funny line.

While psychological pauses create tension and heighten curiosity, logical pauses, between both words and sentences, are more about giving the audience *the time required* for key pieces of information to register and "harden" in their minds.

As with everything, it's a balance. If you pause too briefly between jokes, you run the risk of frustrating laughter. And if you plant pauses that seem too large and obvious, pauses that suggest "insert laughter here," you can come across as if you are asking for their laughter, which again, can really put a crowd off. But make no mistake, pauses are as important as words, just as the blank spaces between the objects in a painting are as important as the objects themselves. Pauses and words, they define each other. Add to those two the idea of emphasis (words spoken with a sense of heightened importance) and you have *three* kinds of sound:

1. silence (pauses)
2. words
3. emphasized words.

Take the following short joke for example.

"I don't have any kids.*// I had a couple of the* neighbor's *but I gave them back."*

In the set-up the word "kids" is emphasized, and in the punchline the word "neighbor's" is emphasized. Note that the pause between the set-up and the punchline is a *two-beat pause.* Unlike a single-beat pause, pausing two beats gives the impression that you are about to move onto another thought. Perhaps related, but not directly connected to what you just said. The fact that the narrative of the punchline turns out to be a direct continuation of the narrative of the set-up adds to the overall surprise of the punchline.

Also note that I *do not* suggest even a single-beat pause between the emphasized word "neighbor's" and the rest of the punchline. If you don't deliver this particular punchline in an uninterrupted stream, the audience may well "get ahead" of you, and start laughing before you get to the words "gave them back." In that case, you'll be talking through the laugh, which can seriously diminish it. And finally, I wouldn't pronounce the words "gave them" as two separate words. I'd just say "gave'em" as one word. Remember, the shorter the punchline, the better.

REPETITION

Another way comics sometimes highlight or emphasize a key piece of information is through repetition rather than pausing. Instead of planting a pause after saying the line, they *repeat* the line or perhaps just the last few words of the line.

"When it comes to understanding math, I figure there's only three kinds of people in the world, three kinds . . ."

When you first try this it may feel a bit unnatural or forced, but if you listen carefully to people talk, you'll notice that they repeat words and even entire sentences much more often than you might imagine. Screenwriter David Mamet makes great use of this natural tendency in his dialogue.

OMITTING WORDS

"Less is more."

—Mies van der Rohe

During everyday conversation, not only do we repeat ourselves much more than you might expect, but we also omit words. This common habit of speech is of particular interest to stand-up comics, who are forever looking for ways to make their jokes as short and as effective as possible.

Obviously if the word conveys a key piece of information for a joke, it can't be omitted. But our language is full of small, almost incidental words and phrases that a comic can leave out or quickly pass over in his delivery. For example, in the set-up of a joke, instead of saying,

"The other day I was walking down the street and I saw this guy and I said to him, 'Look . . .'"

Depending on your style of delivery, you may well be able to merely say,

"Other day/ walking down the street/ saw this guy and I said, 'Look . . .'"

Twenty words versus thirteen words. Seven words axed. That's the kind of editing stand-up is all about.

TIMING

If delivery is *how* a comic says a joke, timing is *when*. And if delivery is difficult to discuss, timing is almost impossible. Timing is about tempo, rhythm. Comics who have great timing are usually comics who speak in a rhythm, a mixture of sounds and silence, that is not only very listenable but also affecting. Their timing makes you *want* to laugh. Something about their rhythm, either its steadiness or, at times, its very unsteadiness, primes the listener to laugh. Like sexual intercourse, it's not just the establishing of certain rhythms that is pleasing, but also the unexpected variations on these established rhythms.

Great timing has a seductive, compelling quality. The Pied Piper played and the rats followed. Just as "music hath charms to soothe the savage breast," great comedic timing hath charms to excite the savage breast to laughter. I know I'm being a little vague, but like I said, timing is a very mysterious thing. And make no mistake, timing can dramatically affect your work. Some comics have great timing and very mediocre material, but they do well because of their *timing*. Other comics have mediocre timing but great material, so they do well because of their *material*. Remember, it all comes down to making the very most of your natural abilities.

Swearing

Individual expression is the beginning and end of all art.
　　　　　　　　　　　　　　　　　—*Proverbs in Prose*

In the world of stand-up comedy, few issues have inspired more heated discussions than that of swearing. Curse words. Profanity. You know what the fuck I mean. To me, swear words can be a very efficient and effective way of conveying an *extreme degree of emotion*. I also use them a fair bit, in my language offstage. So in a sense, when I swear onstage, I think there's a degree of honesty to it that I believe is important. And comedy is all about challenging convention and provoking people. Also, in certain particularly gritty venues (biker bars come to mind), I believe swearing can add a certain credibility to one's presence onstage.

On the other hand, and this is a very important point, if the *only* reason people laugh at a particular joke is because of the shock of a suddenly said curse word, if there's no funny idea behind the joke, then to my mind it's, well . . . bullshit. Yes, I believe in the use of a well-placed swear word if it can goose the laugh of an *already funny* joke, especially if it suits the subject of the joke or the tone of the joke. But I personally do not believe in swearing if the joke is too weak to stand on its own merit and requires a cheap shock technique to get any kind of laugh whatsoever. It's an unartful, band-aid solution, a crutch to a joke that should either be rewritten or put out of its misery.

Some people say, "Really good comics don't have to swear to be funny," and while I think there is some truth to the idea behind this, I think it is a relatively ignorant over-simplification. Yes, if people only laugh when you are swearing, I would agree that you are a severely limited comic, and there will be some situations where you will not be able to do what you do—on a lot of television shows, for example. But if, instead of having to swear to be funny, you choose to use some swear words because you believe they best convey the *feeling* and *content* of what you want to say, I believe it's quite another matter.

An even more important issue than "to swear or not to swear" is the question, "If I'm going to swear, *when* should I swear, and *why* should I swear?" For me, the question of swearing is really a question of *emphasis*. Swearing has a socially perpetuated taboo around it. It has a power, an energy to it. So when I swear, it is usually to emphasize something. But you can't emphasize everything. That would be like a novel written entirely in capital letters. That would be to waste the power of capital letters. But to every now and then put a word in capitals, well, that can be very POWERFUL. A fine tool. No better or worse than any other, especially if used intelligently.

SHOCK COMEDY

"Shock Comedy" is usually a negative label put on a certain comedic style, a style in which the comic provokes the crowd in what some say is an unimaginative, unintelligent, "easy" fashion. For example, many people would consider a comic telling jokes about having sex with young children to be shock comedy. But again, as with all labeling, I believe this might well say more about the labeler than about what he is labeling.

As with the use of swear words, I believe the use of shocking subjects or a shocking style is not so much a matter of whether it's "good" or "bad," "easy" or "hard," as it is of whether it is done well or not. And ultimately, of whether it is *funny* or not. If people laugh at it, it is funny. If they do not, you will be hard pressed to make a living with it, at least as a comic.

FEELING THREATENED

One of the keys to surprising or shocking people in a way that results in laughter is to try to challenge people *without making them feel threatened.* This can be a real tightrope walk, because if you don't run the risk of threatening them, of really challenging their prejudices, then you may well not create enough tension to generate big, loud laughs. Also, if your comedy isn't really challenging people, presenting some fresh and sometimes shocking ideas to them, your material may be derivitive, unoriginal pap. I sometimes think if every joke a comic tells doesn't run the risk of offending *someone,* then maybe it doesn't really express a unique perspective, a real value or belief.

TASTE

Nothing is more personal than taste, and perhaps that is what everything boils down to. Taste. Some stuff tastes "good" to some folks and "bad" to others. For me, at this point in my life and evolution, I would rather do a joke about farting than a joke founded on a gender-based generalization, like "All men are like this" or "All women are like this." It's just right now where my personal taste and belief system are at. Every comic does what he does, usually what he or she finds funny and/or thinks an audience is going to find funny. All a comic can do is perform stuff he thinks people might enjoy, and people will either like it or they won't.

PROVOCATIVE MATERIAL

People often assume that a comedy club is essentially a place where performers *make fun* of stuff, and making fun of something is very close to being disrespectful of it. This is why, no matter how much of a disclaimer a comic may make, some crowds will not respond well to jokes about religion, especially *their* religion. Thankfully, there are definite exceptions to this rule, and some comics have in fact become famous as a result of their religious material. But people's hesitancy to laugh at religious stuff is something you may want to keep in mind, particularly when working a venue far, far away from a "big, bad city."

I don't believe that when you make a joke about something you are always being disrespectful of it. Sure, the chances are you are not being reverential, but I don't think it follows that therefore you must be saying it's full of shit. Comedy is just not that simple. But, as someone very interested in being truly *understood* by an audience, I do try to keep commonly held prejudices in mind.

DELIVERING RISKY JOKES

So you've written some stuff about cutting off the head of the President of the United States with a butter knife and using it as a hand puppet at a children's birthday party.

Or you've got a kooky ten minutes combining elements of necrophilia, pedophilia, and the Holocaust. How should you deliver it?

You may want to try saying it with an "I know this is a little much" attitude. This can be a way of acknowledging the strangeness of the material (so that the club manager doesn't call the police) while at the same time signaling to the crowd that you realize you are probably pushing it when it comes to their trust but sure would appreciate it if they stayed on the bus at least until the next stop. If instead of subtly acknowledging the probable limits to the crowd's trust you just go ahead and talk about the blood-stained butter knife like it's a joke about bad airline food, the audience may well feel obliged to let you know *exactly* how they feel, and, as the outraged patrons rush the stage the club manager may lose confidence in your abilities. Not a good thing.

But there's an old saying in the theater, "Never take the begging bowl onstage." In other words, show no fear. Do not ask them for their approval. Act as if everything's fine. Keep in mind, there is a very thin line indeed between seeming brave and confident and seeming brash and inconsiderate, like you do not care about the audience's feelings. Onstage, you have the power you do because the audience has *given it to you*. Act ungratefully or suggest you don't care about their feelings, and they will take that power back. Quickly.

GROANS

Some comics like getting groans from a crowd; some comics don't. I myself prefer laughter, but a groan *is* a reaction. And at least it's not a "Boo!" or a shout for a refund. Typically, a comic will get a groan from a crowd not just for a bad pun or a corny joke but also for doing provocative material. It's as if the crowd doesn't feel comfortable enough to laugh, but they also don't want the moment to pass without giving some kind of response.

ESTABLISH TRUST FIRST

Trust—the audience's belief in the performer—may well be the most important thing that can exist between the comic and the crowd. Belief and respect, not just in his ability to be funny but also in his respect for them. In that sense, trust is truly a two-way street. For this reason, if you're going to deliver some risky material, jokes you suspect the crowd may not be completely comfortable with, it's a good idea to do so *later* in your set.

I've seen many (usually less experienced) comics begin their routines with risky material (often deliberately trying to be shocking) and immediately lose the crowd. Unlike opening with an unoffensive joke that isn't funny, if you start with a potentially offensive joke and it bombs, you may not be able to get the crowd back. So try to establish some trust first. Some juries take three seconds to convene and refuse to be overturned. Imagine inviting a woman out for dinner and, on your way to the restaurant, you grab her behind. Probably way too much, way too soon. Give both of you a little time to get to know each other first.

HAPPY

MANIC DEPRESSIVE

PARANOID

SCHIZOPHRENIC

MIDGET

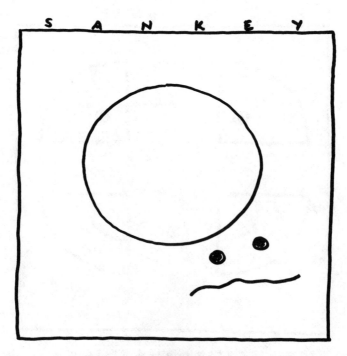

LEPER

MARCEL MARCEAU

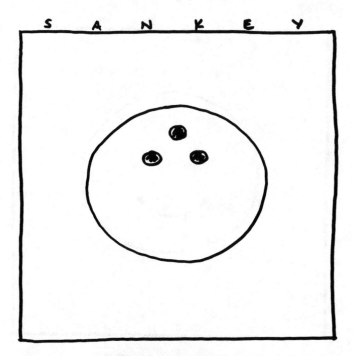

BOWLING BALL

CINDY CRAWFORD

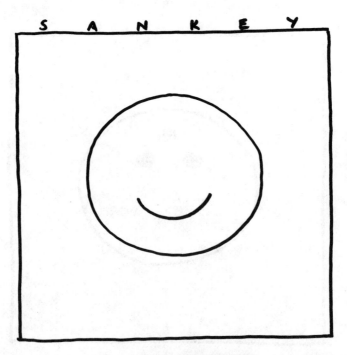

STEVIE WONDER

CHAPTER FIVE

PERFORMANCE

THE TOOLS OF THE TRADE

MICROPHONE AND STAND

The microphone or mike is a comic's best friend. As important as it is for people in the audience to be able to see you, it's even more important that they can *hear* you. That's why, if you're performing in a bar with poor stage lighting, but there's a decent sound system, the show can often go fine. Generally, you should hold the mike two to six inches away from your mouth, but you'll have to hold it much closer for many sound effects (pops, whistles, etc.).

You'll also often have to hold the mike right up to your mouth (sometimes called "eating" the mike) if you find yourself working with a sound system dating back to the Big Band era. This is one of the reasons real professionals watch the other comics on the show before they themselves take the stage, to gauge the power of the mike.

Some comics leave the mike in the stand so that both hands are free to visually act out and emphasize a million and one details in their jokes. Other comics prefer to prowl the stage with mike in hand. Beginners should try both and see which feels most comfortable. As always, experiment.

The ultimate goal of using a mike is for everyone in the audience to be able to hear the subtleties of your voice without them having to strain their ears, or you your voice. And though audiences are more likely to associate confidence with a loud voice than a quiet one, yelling can be fatal. Strive for a voice as clear and engaging as it is powerful, but also a voice that is relaxed and effortless. Remember, pronounced effort in any aspect of performance not only is often distracting but also can send a signal of insecurity and lack of control to the audience.

LIGHTS

There are two kinds of lights in the world of stand-up comedy: white lights and red lights. White lights light the stage, red lights tell you when it's time to get the hell off the stage.

In comedy clubs, you will almost always have excellent stage lighting, but outside of them, you just never know what you'll be working with. This is another reason to watch the comic on stage before you. If you're working a bar gig with mediocre lighting and you see the comic moving in and out of a bright spot, take note of it, and try to stay in the spot when you go up onstage. Unfortunately, the better lit the stage, the hotter it's going to be and the more you may sweat. But again, take note of this *before* you go onstage—and if necessary, have some paper napkins handy.

As for red lights, you'll only find these in comedy clubs, usually located near the back of the room. The red light is flicked on to let a comic know when his time is up, and usually only the club manager has the authority to turn it on. If you see the light come on, it's a *very* good idea to wrap up your set as soon as possible. Trust me.

WRIST WATCH

Time flies when you're having fun.
                                              —Unknown

My third or fourth time onstage I went over my alotted time by a few minutes without even realizing it . . . and found out the hard way. Suddenly, over the speakers came this loud booming voice, "This is the voice of God! Get off the stage!" I hadn't spotted the flashing red light, and the guy in the sound booth had decided to have a little fun. I ran off stage flustered and upset and the very next day bought a wrist watch with a digital stop watch. And believe me, I've been a time-sensitive comic ever since.

I'm forever being amazed by how many so-called pro-fessionals offer "I didn't have a watch" as an explanation for why they did substantially more than their alotted time onstage. I figure, being aware of the time is something you owe not just to the other comics on the show but to the crowd as well. If your sleeves are up, you shouldn't have a problem secretly glancing at your watch from time to time. But try not to get caught looking at your watch. It breaks the magic spell of live performance, reminding the crowd that, as engrossed as they are, time is still passing and they have lives and commitments outside of the club.

GLASS OF WATER

I never go onstage without a glass of water. Apart from keeping your whistle wet, taking a sip of water can be a wonderful stage device, giving your audience a little more time to get a particularly subtle joke or catch their breaths after a particularly funny one. Taking a drink of water can also "plant" a nice pause between a set-up and punchline, or serve as a segue into a bit about water pollution, soft drinks, liquor, water beds, sore throats, etc. And if you happen to have a set list sitting on the stool beside the water, taking a sip gives you the perfect opportunity to take a quick glance.

SET LIST

This is basically a paper napkin, a file card, or a slip of paper with a list of your jokes written on it in the order that you plan to perform them. Comics typically refer to the jokes with just one or two words and write the list in simple block letters. Some comics glance over the list just before going onstage, while other comics take the stage with the list in hand, and then nonchalantly (that is, without chalance) place the list on the stool along with their glass of water. Apart from when you go for a sip of water, a good time to glance at your set list is when your hands are acting something out and your head is tilted down slightly as if to watch your hands. During such moments, you can usually take a nice solid look at your list. But do everything you can not to get caught looking at the list. That can seriously undermine the important illusion of spontaneity.

A danger of set lists is that you can become dependent on them. That can seriously inhibit your desire to improvise, not just material, but even the order of your material. But the virtue of a set list is that you can have definite control of the direction and rhythm of your set. I also find that if you want to try out some new material and you write it as part of your set list (let's say jokes Number Five and Number Seven), you tend to always deliver the new stuff whether the crowd's really with you or not. Without a set list, if the crowd is mediocre many comics balk at breaking in the new stuff, which can be a real loss.

STOOL

Without a stool or chair onstage, it can be pretty difficult to effectively use a set list. I also don't really like having to put my glass of water down onto the stage or even on a nearby table. I like everything handy. For these reasons, I always make sure there's *something* onstage. Some performers also like to actually sit on the stool during part of their set. Being seated can limit the full use of your body, but it can also come across to the crowd as very relaxed and confident. Bill Cosby uses this technique to marvelous effect.

TAPE RECORDER

I believe taping your sets, especially during your first couple of years, is *absolutely essential*. If you're serious about learning stand-up, you'll invest in a small tape recorder. While onstage, so much is going on inside your head and heart that, when you get offstage, don't expect to remember any strong new line you might have "riffed." But if you tape your sets and religiously listen to them despite the boredom of listening to the same jokes over and over, you can learn a great deal about what you said and *how you said it*. You can also learn a lot about the subtle differences between the crowd's reactions to different jokes. In fact, taping your sets is no less than getting a second chance to learn from a single experience. And if you listen to yourself (and the audience) with an ear that's both gentle *and* critical, you can get honest, valuable feedback in a way unlike any other. On top of everything else, listening to yourself over and over will also help a lot when it comes to memorizing the exact wording of your jokes.

Another reason to own a tape recorder is to carry it around and record joke ideas. In many ways, I think this is superior to simply writing ideas down on a piece of paper. Think of it this way. Hearing a spontaneous, naturally created joke pop out of your mouth in conversation is like a fresh flower suddenly appearing out of thin air. As comics, when we grab a pen and jot the joke down, it's like we pressed the vital flower in a book, flattening it, draining it of all the subtle richness of that first intonation, and the rhythm of that first utterance.

If instead you reach for a tape recorder, you probably won't be able to record the joke in all the richness it had when you first said it, but it will be closer than if you simply write it down. And then, when you later have to transcribe the material from tape recorder to some kind of written record, it's a perfect opportunity to edit the joke, which again can only serve to make you a better stand-up comic.

Show and Tell

Don't give a performance. Let the performance give you.
—Sanford Meisner

Another way of looking at the difference between traditional actors and comics is that actors in a play try to *show* a story, while stand-up comics try to *tell* a story. Actors demonstrate what they are thinking and feeling, while most comics tend to describe their thoughts and feelings.

This view of the stand-up comic as a "teller" is certainly the traditional view, but there are many comics, some of the most successful in fact, who strive to make their performances as much about showing as they are about telling. These comics embody a more theatrical approach to stand-up by not only using their faces, hands, and bodies to flesh out their jokes, and by expressing a greater range of emotions in their work, but also by occasionally using props and music as well. The result is a style of stand-up that is much more inherently engaging to watch than the traditional "talking head" approach, especially to modern audiences weaned on television.

Memory

When playing a game of pinball, you can gently shake the machine, but if you jiggle if too hard and cause the machine to tilt the game shuts down. I believe that when we laugh hard at something, it's like a momentary tilt to the human memory. Laughter, especially hard sudden laughter, is a shock to the system, momentarily impairing one's attention span, even one's memory. It's for this reason that magicians often do "the secret move" when an audience is laughing. It also explains why people sometimes forget the punchline to a joke.

Another way to imagine this is to think of the human consciousness as a bucket of water. When the person is listening to someone, each word the other person says is like a tiny bead dropped into the bucket, sending gentle ripples across the surface of the water. A sudden, surprising, strong joke, however, is more like dropping a large stone than a bead into the water, jarring the bucket and creating much larger ripples.

TAKING THE STAGE

The MC has just said your name, the audience is applauding, you are stepping onto the stage (and hopefully you have just checked your watch to monitor your time!). There is a perfect moment to say your first word, a sweet spot, sometime between the applause dying out and a definite silence settling in. It can't be described so much as *felt*, but you'll know when you hit it. If you speak too soon, you can seem unrelaxed, overeager. Then again, if you speak too late you can seem unsure or nervous.

Try to arrive onstage full of thoughts and feelings, focused on your first joke, carrying yourself as if you have something you want to share with the crowd. But beware giving the impression that, as you speak your first sentences, you are "beginning" something. For your character onstage to be perfectly credible, it is a better idea to try to give the impression that you are simply *continuing* something, something that goes on offstage as much as it does onstage.

CONTINUING VS. BEGINNING

Don't come onstage empty.

—Sanford Meisner

As you wait to take the stage, focus on your character. Try to imagine how he might feel, and what he might be thinking about it, if he had been invited to give a talk at a comedy club and was just about to take the stage. Think (and feel) about your first joke in particular, and your desire to share in general. After all, on a certain level, the *desire to share* is one of the few things all performers have in common. Whatever else they are motivated by, if they have shown up for the performance, they probably want to share something.

Also, as I've mentioned several times, the illusion of spontaneity is very important to a stand-up performance, so when first taking the stage and beginning to speak, you do not want to give the impression of beginning a prewritten monologue. Strive instead to give the impression that yes, you have begun to share your thoughts and feelings with the audience, but the thoughts and feelings have been with you all day. Try to take the stage with the attitude that "there is something I'd like to tell you." The goal is for people in the audience to leave the club assuming that you are "always like that," and that who you are onstage is a *continuation* of who you are offstage. Remember, art and illusion go hand in hand.

WHAT SHOULD I DO WITH MY HANDS?

This is a more common question than you might imagine. More often than not, being unusually aware of your hands is an expression of general discomfort and nervousness rather than a true awkwardness about your hands. In time, not only will you stop being conscious of your hands, but with a little practice your hands will move in 101 ways to support visually whatever you're talking about.

There's no question that some people are more naturally expressive with their hands than others, but either way you would do well to experiment with your hands as much as possible. They are, after all, communication tools capable of

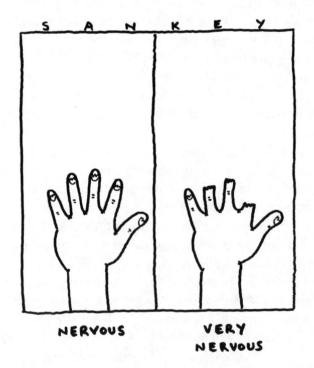

NERVOUS   VERY
                       NERVOUS

great sophistication, and making the most of whatever tools you have is what excellent stand-up is all about. Just watch Robin Williams, Jim Carrey, or even the more physically subtle Dennis Miller. They all make marvelous use of their hands to bring their jokes, and their characters, to *life*.

GETTING THEM

Take to the stage as a bird to the air. It is your medium.
—Sanford Meisner

I have to admit that, for some reason, it wasn't until my third or fourth year as a stand-up comic that I started to realize just how important it is, at the beginning of your set, to do whatever it takes to "get" the crowd. Don't get me wrong. Up until then, I had always known that your first few jokes have to be strong, but I tended to put more thought into *keeping* a crowd rather than *getting* them.

But then, right after a particularly strong performance at a comedy festival, it dawned on me that I hadn't just walked on that stage with a smile on my face. I had "taken" that stage. From the very first moment of the set, I hadn't just been completely focused on being there, I had also somehow asserted my presence to the entire audience. I know it sounds a little hocus pocus, but those are the best words I can come up with to describe my experience.

And the way I went into my first joke . . . I had some-how started speaking at the perfect time. A beat after the audience applause had died down but just before any real silence had set in. I hit the sweet spot, and rather than my first joke being an absolute beginning, it felt more like a continuation of the energy of the applause. Of course, at the time I wasn't aware of any of this, but afterwards it occurred to me that it had been a kind of watershed set for me. A new beginning. So now, more than ever, as truly important as it is to open a set with material that is strong, accessible, and has broad appeal, I try also to focus on both the *energy* and the *attitude* required to really GET a crowd, right off the bat.

KEEPING THEM

The only thing that keeps the audience in their seats is wondering what's going to happen next.

—David Mamet

Despite the fact that you've told the same jokes a hundred times, at its best performing is much more a matter of *creation* than re-creation. Every time you take the stage, you must, in a sense, raise the dead. The jokes, the funny faces, and the apparently off-the-top-of-your-head quips you've done a zillion times are all well-worn ghosts of the past. But tonight you must make them breathe and dance again. To accomplish such a feat requires nothing less than an *investment of your life energy*, and it is to that very investment that an audience will respond most. That's what keeps a crowd there, in the palm of your hand. Vitality, life.

But we all get tired, even a little bored with our material. Every performer you've ever seen has had nights where he just didn't feel like doing it. Not again, not tonight. So, he "phones in" his set, merely goes through the motions, and if he's a seasoned pro he'll probably get away with it. But it's just not the same. The truly great performers somehow find what it takes to, more often than not, make a real emotional investment in their material, their schtick.

CONNECTING

The practice of Zen is forgetting the self in the act of uniting with something.

—Koun Yamada

Just as it's essential to connect with your character and your material, it's important to connect with the audience. To really *be there* for them. I once saw a magician before a show jumping up and down in the washroom, saying out loud, "I love my audience! I love my audience!" (Needless to say, it was a bit weird.) A more common approach to the idea of connecting with an audience is to always be sending "positive threads of energy" from your eyes out to every corner of the club. Of course this is a physical metaphor for a psychological or spiritual act, but such concepts can be an effective way of gathering and focusing your energy. Another thought I often keep in mind, something I once heard an actor say, is, "Always be letting them know they are welcome in your theater." To me, this nicely sums up the core feeling of being connected with the audience.

Comics often say, "Play to the back of the room," the idea being that if you make a strong effort to reach and involve the people at the back of the room, you will probably connect with the people closer to the stage as well. On a more physical level, to connect with a crowd you should at the very least always be smoothly turning your body from left to right, then back again. That way, though the people to the extreme right and left of the stage won't actually be seeing your full face as often as the people directly in front of the stage, you will at least be giving them a good look at it on a *regular basis*.

ENERGY

You only get out of it what you put into it.

—Unknown

It's a cliché (but that doesn't make it any less true) that performing for a good crowd is a lot like having good sex. It takes two. Your energy and theirs. It's all a matter of give and take. Real pros fill the room with their energy, magically knitting the crowd together, gathering them into their spell, moulding them, apparently effortlessly, into a single, living unit. An Audience. But more often than not, whether it is subtly asserted or dramatically declared, it all begins with the power of the comic's energy.

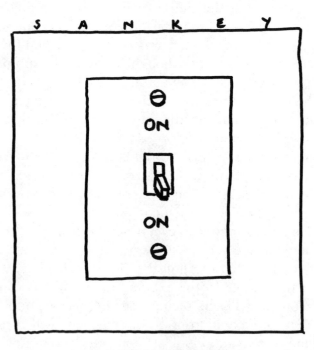

NYMPHOMANIAC

Whether you see the performer as the wick and the crowd as the dynamite, or the crowd as the wick and the performer as the dynamite, invariably it is the performer that is expected to provide the match. That first spark is up to you. So don't wait for them to come to you. *Take your show to them.* And keep in mind that, as with most things, the Law of Diminishing Returns applies. If you give them 50 percent, you'll often only get 20 percent or 30 percent in return. So when you take the stage, try to give them all the energy you can. More often than not, it's worth it. Like I said, performing for a good crowd is a lot like having good sex. And you even get paid for it!

SHOW YOUR NECK

Animals in the wild usually protect their necks, sensing that they are risking their lives whenever they openly expose them. In fact, I've read that when two animals meet in the forest for the first time (let's say two foxes that have never met before), they sometimes go through a subtle, instinctive dance, taking turns showing more and more of their necks before they fully relax in each other's presence. Remind you of something?

If you want an audience to trust you, to go along with you even as you head into provocative areas, to in a sense show you their necks, it's a good idea to *first show them yours.* This is one of the reasons you should try to cultivate a subtle sense of vulnerability in your stage character. Let them see that you really don't think you're perfect. Let them see that you can be hurt, and that you too have your sensitive areas. But beware trying to show them too much of your neck too soon. Even this takes time. Think twice about opening your set with your saucy "fucking Dad in the sleeping bag" bit. Start slowly, but keep in mind, if you want them to trust you, to show you theirs, it's a good idea to first show them yours.

HAVING FUN ONSTAGE

Just before I go onstage, I often ask one of the other comics, "Any advice?" More often than not, they say, "Don't bomb." The next most common reply is "Have fun." They're both good pieces of advice, but I particularly like the second one. I've said it before; the crowd *looks to you* to see how they should feel about what you are doing and saying, and if you look like you're having fun, they're going to be tempted to join in. God knows it's not always easy to have fun onstage, what with the rough crowds and your own emotional mood swings, but if you can possibly have some fun while you're up there, or even at least look like you're having fun, it will greatly enhance your set. Remember, fun is contagious.

LEAVING THE STAGE

Cue the crowd that you are about to leave before you actually do. Before they deliver their last joke, some comics say something like, "Before I go, I'd just like to . . . ," or "Well, I should probably get going, but before I do . . ." This way, I suspect some people in the crowd think, "Oh, here comes the last joke, I better really pay attention." While others think, "Oh, too bad, he's leaving so soon" and emotionally prepare themselves to thank the comic for making them laugh as much as he did.

This "thanking the comic" is a very important part of the performer/audience dynamic. As a younger comic, I used to bolt from the stage the moment I finished my last joke, probably out of nervousness or doubt. But by doing so, I was stealing from both myself and the audience. I wasn't giving the audience a chance to *express their gratitude* and I wasn't giving myself a chance to *receive it*. I also wasn't giving the audience a chance to see me happily receive their gratitude and gratefully acknowledge it.

If it sounds like a dance, that's because a dance is exactly what it is. Both sides, taking turns, showing signs of respect and empowering each other. And practically speaking, by cueing the crowd to your departure, you also cue the MC to get ready to retake the stage. And if the MC is in the back of the club having a smoke (or out in the alley selling heroin to preschoolers) it gives someone a chance to run and get him.

STRENGTH VS. AGGRESSION

The artist is one who can do more, but doesn't.
—Japanese expression

Some comics seem to be able to calmly take complete control of the situation without even telling a single joke. Other comics hit the stage like a lion, ripping laughs out of the crowd from the very start. As always, there's more than one way to skin a cat (though I wouldn't let the neighbors see you doing it). But generally speaking, good comics have *a relaxed air of strength* about them.

Most pros are strong; far fewer are actually aggressive. The difference is this: Strength suggests, while Aggression shows. Strength silently states, while Aggression shouts. And there's something about shouting that betrays a need, even a fear. And fear is the enemy, especially when it comes to performing. This is true if for no other reason than that audiences will respond far more favorably, far more often, to a show of strength than one of aggression.

So by all means, do everything you can to cultivate a sense of strength when you take the stage, but think twice about being openly aggressive. I've certainly had moments when I've been very aggressive onstage, but after the show, when I've really thought about it, I've usually decided that there was unnecessary insecurity behind it. Only in the last couple of years am I starting to appreciate the power of restraint, of smiling rather than flexing.

CONVICTION

Leap, and the net will appear.

—Actor's expression

The idea of conviction is at the core of how you carry yourself and deliver your material onstage. Though it takes years to be a fine stand-up comic, it's essential that you eventually come to *believe* that you are funny and have a right to be up on that stage, telling jokes in front of all those people. Offstage, a little self-doubt will take you far. But onstage, there's no place for doubt.

But belief in yourself as a comic is not so much something you can work on as it is something that slowly happens, almost without you knowing it, over several years. Unlike bravado and vanity, which are more often signs of insecurity, real belief in one's self takes time and yields a powerful sense of credible conviction onstage that bravado and vanity can't possibly duplicate.

Also, unlike real conviction, bravado betrays its true origins by subtly asking the crowd for something when it says, "Aren't I bold and brash?" Experienced comics never seem to be "asking" the crowd for anything. Not approval, not laugher, nothing. They seem to just be speaking their minds, being who they are. Appearing relaxed and confident, the crowd in turn relaxes, confident that the comic not only is going to be funny, but *is* funny. Consequently, the audience is in the ideal state of mind to laugh and laugh freely.

As actors often say, "Don't take the begging bowl onstage." Everyone in the audience paid to watch you stand up there onstage with the mike and lights. You may well feel the pressure of their expectations, but it is also a kind of power. Trust yourself not only to deserve it, but also to know what to do with it. Relax. As much as you really, really want them to laugh their asses off, try to seem to be asking for nothing. While at the same time, strongly believing they will laugh. Believing in it is very important.

CONTROL

The successful General chooses his own battlefield.
—Military expression

Stand-up comics are often control freaks. Why else would they be drawn to a craft where they get to be everything from the writer and director to the performer and promoter? On the other hand, there is a great deal in a performance of stand-up comedy the comic can't predict, let alone control. The mood of the crowd, the quality of the lights, the loud music from the dance club next door. As a stand-up comic, you just never know what's going to happen, and I suspect that too is one of the things that attracts certain personalities to stand-up.

Who knows, maybe a lot of comics are naturally controlling people, with a longing to be out of control. I know I'm certainly like that. But because there is so much we can't control, I figure comics should control whatever we can. The consistency and credibility of our characters onstage, the clarity of our material, and even the number of minutes we spend onstage (in relation to how long we're supposed to be onstage) are all things we can control. And thus, I believe, we *must*.

Repetition and Stimulation

To be said to have a "style," a comic must in some sense *repeat himself*. The way he delivers his jokes, the subjects he talks about, the way he writes his material, something. So, strictly speaking, repetition is not a bad thing. However, there's a thin line between having a style and being predictable. Always talking about drugs is one thing. Always talking about the very same drug from the very same perspective is another. Variety is essential. But so is a certain amount of consistency, without which the audience won't have a chance to really get into the groove of what you're doing. Also, without some kind of consistency, you're going to have a tough time building credibility and gaining the trust of the crowd, both of which are extremely important. Yet, without variety, you're going to have a hard time keeping the audience stimulated and attentive. It's all about a balance between repetition and stimulation. As always, a tightrope walk.

EFFORT AND GRACE

If one really wishes to master an art, technical knowledge is not enough. One has to transcend technique so that the art becomes an "artless art" growing out of the Unconscious.
—D. T. Suzuki

"They make it look so easy." We've all heard this said of basketball players, musicians, and, yes, even stand-up comics (though never accountants) and it's almost always a testament to years and years of committed, disciplined practice. But it's not like, when they started, any of them knew exactly what it was going to take to get where they are. If they did, I suspect more than a few of them wouldn't have had the courage to begin. Instead, I bet a lot of them simply followed a dream, a spark, or an obvious aptitude . . . and hoped for the best.

To become really good at almost anything worth being good at, you have to work at it pretty much every day. And one of life's little ironies is that as you become good at something, *it magically starts to vanish,* to become a part of you, so that you can barely distinguish between it and you. When you start, you're all thumbs. And then, as you begin to get good at it, the thumbs vanish one-by-one. In the end, once you're truly proficient at it, you wake up one day and find yourself with what appears to be your same old pair of hands: eight fingers, two thumbs. But there's no comparison between what they can do now and what they could do then. This is why it's often said that "great art is the concealing of art," leaving one with an amazing effortlessness. Remember, it took Jim Carrey fifteen years to become an "overnight success." In the end, there seems to be only one way to become excellent at something, and make it look so damn easy, and that's by working so damn hard.

WHATEVER DOESN'T ADD, DETRACTS

The ability to simplify means to eliminate the unnecessary so that the necessary may speak.
—Hans Hoffman

This applies to performing stand-up no less than it applies to writing stand-up. As important as it is to use your hands, your face, even your legs to bring your material to life, if an action doesn't definitely *add* something effective and relevant to the joke or the bit, it should be mercilessly *dropped*, no matter how much you like it. If it doesn't "goose the laugh" or clarify a point or image, get rid of it. Stuff that doesn't add not only detracts, it often distracts as well. Just as when you sometimes discover you can remove a sentence from a joke without losing the laugh, if you can drop a hand gesture or a facial expression without harming the joke, drop it. Don't clutter up the eyes of the audience with useless, unnecessary stuff!

READING ONSTAGE

Most of the time, comics try to achieve the illusion of talking off the tops of their heads, sharing an unrehearsed series of ideas with the crowd. But as always, there are exceptions. One of these is when the performer reads something to the audience, usually a poem or a story or something from a magazine or newspaper. Actually, you won't see this done very often, and for at least a couple of good reasons.

One reason is that, after seeming to be "just talking" for fifteen or twenty minutes, for you to then take a piece of paper out of your pocket and start reading, you run a real risk of reminding the crowd that it's a show after all, which can undercut the crowd's suspension of disbelief. Another reason is that shifting the focus from the audience watching and listening to you, to really just listening to you read something, can break the general flow of your set. And, considering that your eyes are among *your most powerful communication tools*, used to both connect with the audience and hold its attention, to do something that requires you to turn your eyes away from the crowd to read, can be dangerous.

But still, many performers, including myself, do read stuff onstage. I've even known comics who routinely take a sheet of paper up onstage with them, and simply read off a dozen jokes without really putting much energy into the performance or delivery. Their thinking is that, rather than putting in the time and energy it takes to write, memorize, rehearse, and really *perform* twelve new jokes onstage (only to find out five of them "fly") they just read the jokes to the crowd, figuring that any joke that gets a good laugh when merely being read will get a *big* laugh when actually performed.

I think there's a lot of truth to this, but I also think it limits the kind of joke the comic will eventually perform. Jokes that get laughs when just being read out loud are clearly not dependent on stuff like facial expressions, position in the set, or character in general, at least not to any great extent. So though I think it can be a very efficient way to arrive at a kind of knowledge, I still think it's very limiting and certainly doesn't do much to help hone your performing skills.

BREAKING IN NEW MATERIAL

New material can be scary, but it can also be a great deal of fun. Seasoned professionals often say that it's the new stuff that keeps them fresh onstage, perking up a whole set and almost forcing them to be psychologically really there onstage. To me, a new joke is like a newborn baby. Beautiful, but also sensitive and fragile. So I literally "baby" new material by trying it out in front of a friendly, receptive crowd whenever possible. I also try to avoid opening my set with new material. My thinking is that, for the new stuff to get a real chance, for you to get a valid read on how strong or weak it is, it's best if the crowd *already believes you are funny* before you try the new stuff.

There are two reasons for this. First, if you've already proven you're funny, and then try new stuff that goes down like the Hindenburg, you'll probably be able to get the crowd back with tried-and-true material. But if you open your set with new stuff that bombs, you haven't built up any trust with the crowd, and even when you go to your stronger material it may be a bit of an uphill climb. Second, expecting a new joke to carry the burden of opening your set is, to my mind, not giving it a fair chance. Unless of course the new bit *must* be used as an opener. I tend to try new material somewhere *in the middle of my set*, sandwiched between more seasoned pieces. That way, not only does the new stuff get a real chance to fly (being delivered to a fully primed crowd), but if it doesn't go over well, I can quickly get the crowd back with the seasoned stuff that follows it.

I also don't think there's much point in doing too much new material all at once, new joke after new joke. Here's why. Let's say the first new joke goes over well—fine. But then, let's say the second and third new joke that immediately follow both die a horrible death. Now, if you go into a fourth new joke, it's got to carry the burden of the two stinkers before it. Not a very nice thing to do to a brand new baby joke. That's why I try to never deliver more than two new jokes in a row, before going back to some tried-and-true stuff.

It's important to try out new material as often as possible, especially during your first few years in the business. You could stick to the same stuff show after show, and still learn a lot about timing and stage presence, but after six or seven years onstage, very few successful comics use any of the jokes they wrote in their first two years. Those jokes simply aren't strong enough, not compared to the stuff they write as they get more experienced.

How many times should you tell a joke that continues to get a poor or "soft" response? As always, this differs from comic to comic. I know comics who, if they really like a joke, will continue to do the joke no matter what the audience reaction, even if the joke bombs half the time. This doesn't make much sense to me. On the other hand, neither does it make much sense to me only to try a new joke once and, if it doesn't fly, discard it. After investing the time it took to write the joke and then perform it, such a demanding attitude can be a real waste.

New jokes deserve a chance to "get their legs," and this requires the comic saying the joke onstage in front of a crowd at least a few times. My own rule is sometimes two times, usually three, and occasionally four. If I toss out a new bit to a piping hot crowd that's laughing hard at absolutely everything up to that point . . . and the joke gets nothing, complete silence, I am *very* suspicious of it. But maybe something was off with my delivery or I have to reword the joke to make it a little clearer, so I'll often try the joke once more. If I try a new joke in front of a crowd and it gets a couple of chuckles, I'll be more apt to believe that the joke might eventually get its legs, and I'll be willing to try it three times before deciding whether to keep it or chuck it. And if I really, really like a joke, if I'm convinced it's got great potential, I might try four times before deciding, after four soft audience responses, to trash it. Remember, there are millions of jokes out there waiting to be conceived, and stage time is too precious to waste on weak material. It comes down to the survival of the fittest. Or at least, the funniest.

DEALING WITH NERVES

If a man wishes to be sure of the road he treads on, he must close his eyes and walk in the dark.

—Saint John of the Cross

EATING BEFORE THE SHOW

Very few comics say they like to eat a big meal just before they go onstage. A lot of comics say they give their best performances on an empty stomach. And many even go so far as to say they like to take the stage directly following a triumphant bowel movement. For me, I find eating a meal around an hour and a half before I take the stage is just perfect. I don't have a full stomach, but I still have some energy to burn. On a night with two shows, I'll either eat between shows or eat a couple of hours before the first show and then maybe grab a chocolate bar between shows.

SWEATING (AND YOU WILL)

Sweating onstage lets the crowd know you're working hard for them.

—Jerry Lewis

Whether because of nerves, the temperature of the room, or something eaten for dinner, sooner or later we all sweat onstage. And though I don't completely disagree with Mr. Lewis, I also believe that seeing a comic sweat can sometimes send the wrong message to a crowd. That's why I always have a handkerchief in my pocket onstage. Not only because I happen to do a couple of quick little bits with it, but also because if I start to sweat, I'd rather wipe my brow with a clean hanky than a stained beer coaster. And if you're wearing a jacket, don't hesitate to stop and take a moment to take it off. Not only is it a completely natural thing to do, but it can send a real message of being "casual and relaxed" to the crowd.

I read somewhere that one of the best ways to keep sweating to a minimum is to drink a lot of water. Sounds a bit backwards, but I've tried it and it seems to work (at least a little). I also read that, apparently, hot liquids actually cool your system down better than cold liquids. I admit I don't feel much like a cup of tea or boiling chicken fat just before hitting the stage, but I do try to make a point of taking a glass of *room temperature* water, rather than cold, up onstage with me. That way, too, no condensation forms on the glass and leaves big, wet rings on my set list.

Also, if you're sweating, you may simply be going too fast. Going too fast is much more common than going too slowly. Between the crowd's alcohol intake, its different levels of intelligence, and the fact that, unlike you,

CABBIE ON A DATE

they haven't heard your jokes a thousand times, it's almost impossible to go too slowly for most crowds, especially if you go at a steady pace.

DOUBT CAN BE GOOD

Everyone gets nervous. In fact, one of humankind's most common fears is standing up in front of a group of people and talking. After hundreds of sets, many comics lose a sense of nervousness, but when just starting out the vast majority of performers are more than a little nervous before every single show. Keep that in mind. You are not alone in your nervousness, and it's *a natural part of the process*. In fact, being nervous before a set can be a very positive sign, indicating that you care strongly about doing well and are unsure about the outcome of your show. This caring, combined with humble uncertainty, makes for the ideal fuel to become a much better comic.

Without this fuel, you actually may not go as far. That's one of the reasons I'm sometimes glad I'm not a more naturally funny person. Seriously. Oh, I was born with my fair share of wit, but I'm nowhere near as naturally funny as some comics I know. They're just naturally funny guys. Laughs come easy to them, so they don't really have to work at it. And as a result . . . some of them *don't* work at it, and their craft suffers for it. So take heart if you're unsure of some of your abilities and feel compelled to push yourself to succeed. In the long run, there's no substitute for hard work, caring strongly about what you do, and a healthy dose of self-doubt. But note, there is an important difference between a little stage anxiety and nervousness that results from the suspicion that one is *inadequately prepared*. If you haven't rehearsed in days or written in weeks, your anxiety is a warning: Get to work!

TONIGHT DOESN'T MATTER

Nervous energy can also be an excellent source of fuel onstage, especially if you learn how to make it work for you rather than against you. One way to avoid being completely debilitated by your quaking nerves is to try to keep things in perspective. Everyone bombs and has the occasional soft set. I try to think of the pains of a poor set as birthing pains. We tend to get amazingly egocentric when we bomb, thinking people care about our failure. They don't care, especially on amateur nights. No matter how poorly you did, twenty minutes after you leave the stage people won't remember you or the fact that your new four-minute bit about Greek cattle rustlers didn't get a single laugh. Always remind yourself, "Tonight doesn't really matter. What matters is the performer I'm going to be five years from now." I still tell myself that.

TRY TO RELAX

It's an axiom of many acting techniques that the human body cannot be expressive to the best of its abilities unless it is *relaxed*. So instead of being tense due to nerves, the performer should ideally be relaxed before taking the stage. But you may ask, "If the last three guys onstage all died a horrible death, and I'm up next, how the hell am I supposed to RELAX?" Well, plug your earphones into your tape recorder (which you should have with you to tape your set!) and try listening to some of your favorite music. Some comics have great success with this. Or try finding a spot in the club, perhaps in a back room far from the stage, where you can sit down and really relax. A good rule of thumb for this is to try to find a position in which, if you had to, you could fall asleep. Doing some gentle stetching exercises can also be helpful, and be sure to slowly roll your shoulders several times to loosen any anxiety built up in your neck and shoulders.

WARMING UP

Now is also a good time not only to relax, but also to get your mouth and face loosened up. Repeating simple verbal warm-ups like, "She sells seashells down by the seashore" and "How much wood could a woodchuck chuck if a woodchuck could chuck wood?" are perfect for this. And be sure to work the muscles in your face by pulling a number of funny faces, one after the other. That should help you loosen up your physical self.

As for your mental self, there's an improv game called "Uses" that I often play just before going on. Basically, the game involves picking up an object on hand (pencil, book of matches, etc.) and trying to quickly come up with a series of different imaginary scenarios involving the shape of the object. For example, I grab a pencil and play-act that it's a cigar, then a heroin needle, then a single unbroken eyebrow across my forehead, then a rolling pin, etc. Don't censor yourself, go with whatever comes to mind. This can also be a fun exercise to do with another comic, the two of you quickly passing the object back and forth.

RUN THROUGH YOUR MATERIAL

Many comics try to relax by quickly running through their material just before going onstage. I often do this myself, but I think you should only run through it in your mind, or jot key words down on a piece of paper, or at most, mumble some of it out loud. *Never* find a quiet spot in the club (in the green room, an empty hallway, etc.) and actually "perform" your jokes, saying them out loud with real juice behind them, just before going onstage.

That's what your dress rehearsals are for. Other than those, save the real blood and guts for the stage.

REHEARSING

I rehearse everywhere. In the shower, walking to the store, sitting on the bus, in the laundromat. Sometimes I'll just be running over some new material in my mind. Other times I'll be quietly saying the stuff right out loud. Yeah, I've received more than a few suspicious glances from strangers, but I figure I'm not bothering them, and my progress is worth it. In fact, truth be told, I often think of my creative side as a little baby. My little baby. And it needs food. And though I don't have any real children (yet), I imagine if I did I would do pretty much anything to feed my baby. I try to do the same for my creative side. It deserves no less.

But quietly rehearsing stuff while sitting in a restaurant is not the same as rehearsing your material, at home, alone, in a silent room, delivering your jokes at the volume you do onstage, as well as using your body, your hands, and your face to support the material effectively. When I first started I bought a mike and a mike stand and practiced every day, for at least an hour, in front of a full-length mirror. I'm not saying this approach is going to work for everyone, but I do suggest you at least give it a try. Also, have a glass of water handy, resting on a stool or chair, as well as a pad of paper and a pen. This is not only so you can have a set list, but also because it's during full dress rehearsals that you'll often come up with new tags and bits of business. I know it's a little boring, standing alone in a room, going over the same material again and again, but sometimes that's what it takes to get yourself into a fertile state of mind, almost lulling the conscious mind to relax its grip, allowing the *unconscious mind* to subtly give up its comedic gold.

And be sure to have your watch handy. Though performing your material for a live audience will dramatically affect the amount of time it takes to deliver it, with practice you'll be able to have a pretty good idea of how many minutes of rehearsal equal how many minutes onstage. More than many other crafts, stand-up is *an exacting art of seconds.* Literally, I think you would be wise to always be working toward a greater sensitivity to the passage of time.

By all means, rehearse individual jokes, but rehearsing material in larger chunks, strings of five or six jokes at a time, can magically sand off rough corners between jokes, as you discover smoother segues and a more effective order. You may also want to consider taping the occasional rehearsal. There's no crowd reaction (unless your bedroom is in a train station), but listening to yourself delivering material in a completely silent room can be very educational.

Also, try your best to deliver your material not only at the same volume you use in a club, but at the same speed as well. Some comics have even gone so far as to set up a metronome, having it tick as they rehearse, to aid them in maintaining a steady rhythm to their delivery. And if you're on really good terms with the manager of your local comedy club, you might want to try to do some rehearsing on an actual stage. Just arrive several hours before the show, ideally even before the bar and wait staff show up, ask someone to flick on the stage light, and spend some "private time" onstage. Remember, your goal is nothing less than to feel as comfortable onstage as you do sitting at home in your favorite chair.

Rehearsing on a regular basis will also greatly enhance your memory. Every time you run through your set you are etching your material that much more into your memory. And keep in mind, it's really only once you've got your material down cold, being able to both remember your jokes and deliver them clearly, that you can begin to rise to the much more exciting challenge of *performing*.

PROPS

It does not matter how slowly you go so long as you do not stop.
—Confucius

A handkerchief, a book of matches, a water pistol. Just as music has a unique power and value, so do props. But unlike music (especially intro music, which I believe can be used with great subtlety), when the comic uses a prop onstage, it tends to draw attention to itself. Props, or as I think of them, "prop moments," are interesting because most comics spend most of their time *talking* about stuff, but during a prop moment, it's more about *showing*.

In other words, when a comic tells a joke he is usually sharing a description of an event or an idea. He is sharing it in the Here and Now, but more often than not, the event has already happened. But by introducing a prop and doing something funny with it, the comic moves from describing events to an immediate, vital, real-time *happening*. No translation is required because the comic is not sharing a personal experience with the audience.

Instead, it is a group experience. To me, this experience is the key to whatever power prop moments possess.

In fact, moments involving props can sometimes get such a strong audience reaction that comics who do something funny and memorable with a particular prop often end their show with it. This also makes some sense from the perspective of transitions. Moving from jokes (descriptions) to a prop (a shared experience) heightens the immediacy. To then, after a prop moment, go *back* to jokes, back to mere descriptions, requires the crowd to make yet another transition, which could be dangerous because it's *during transitions that the comic runs the greatest risk of losing focus*, both the audience's and his own.

In my own work I don't have a lot of prop moments, but I do sometimes enjoy throwing one in if only to keep the audience as stimulated as possible. But I also believe prop moments have dangers even apart from the risks of transitions. First, one of the primary goals of traditional stand-up is to seem spontaneous and unprepared. Suddenly pulling a jar of pickles out of your pocket doesn't look very spontaneous. As a result, such things run the risk of weakening the crowd's belief in the comic "speaking off the top of his head."

Also, if not done in a careful fashion, suddenly pulling a jar of pickles out of your pocket can look to the audience like you are *asking for a response*. It can come across as an artless (even desperate) snatch at the crowd's funny bone. An all-too-obvious cue for laughter. And though such bold techniques may work wonders in some situations, in other situations their very boldness will work against the comic. We all know how restrictive it can feel to have someone expect something from us, especially when we aren't sure we want to give it to them. And yet, despite the dangers of prop moments, many very successful comics use the occasional prop, and audiences do seem to appreciate it. Perhaps, handled artfully, the very showiness of props works in favor of the comic. It is, after all, called "show business."

OTHER TALENTS

Do you do a great Clint Eastwood impression? A cool magic trick? Can you juggle? Are you fluent in a dozen languages? Telling really funny jokes in an artful, unique fashion isn't easy, and it usually takes years of practice and experience. But as you become comfortable with the telling of jokes, you may want to experiment with the idea of bringing other talents to the stage. Your act is *you*. It should be a vital, growing thing, and you'll be surprised with just how elastic it can be. With a little faith (and an incredible amount of work) you can incorporate almost anything into your stand-up set. But for it to truly fit into your set, whatever you try will have to be at least one thing: *funny*.

MAGIC TRICKS

I've been fiddling with magic tricks for years, and I have to admit, I've tried to bring some of them to my stand-up set. But so far, I haven't had much success, and I think I know why. When a performer plays a guitar, or juggles some balls, or does an impression of a famous person, nobody in the audience thinks, "How the hell did he do that?" Oh sure, if the performer is very good, people are definitely impressed, in awe of his ability, and might even think, "I could never do that." But, strictly speaking, they are not *fooled* by what he did.

But magic tricks done well do fool people. And because people traditionally see a magic trick as a problem to be solved they are quick to try to see past the trick and invest thought in trying to figure it out. This can really screw up the comedic rhythm between the audience and the comic. Unlike a punchline to a joke, which is often a sudden bringing together of things, *a sudden clarification*, a magic trick is often the opposite, a sudden, unsolvable mystery. And usually, when people are truly puzzled, they don't feel like laughing.

It's a tricky marriage, mystery and laughter, especially if you've just spent twenty minutes developing a comedic rapport and a rhythm with a crowd. In fact, the only comics I've ever seen who use magic effectively in their stand-up acts tend to make a *big joke of the trick*, draining it of almost all its mystery. And I have to admit, having fiddled with magic for as long as I have, I just don't feel right about reducing a good trick to the level of a whoopee cushion. I want to keep the potential for creating wonder in an audience. So thus far I haven't had much success bringing magic tricks to my stand-up . . . but I'm going to keep trying.

MUSIC

Legend has it that a very famous comic was once at a Hollywood party with many of the guests hovering around him, in awe of his fame and in hopes of seeing him say or do something funny. But a few minutes later, when a very famous musician showed up at the party, many of the guests lost interest in the comic and began circling the musician. Whether or not the story is true, I believe there is truth *in it*. People love to laugh—it is a universally cherished experience. But as much as laughter means to them, music seems to mean even more. Flip through almost any newspaper, pick up any magazine, you will find many more references to music than comedy, especially in the North American culture.

Music has tremendous appeal and power, so much so that I am amazed by how few comics use it in their acts. And I don't mean playing an instrument or having the sound guy at the back of the room toss a cassette into the player and doing some physical comedy to a prerecorded song. Very few comics I've met are even interested in making the most of their own intro music—the song playing as they walk onstage. To me, this is a real mistake.

Few things in the human experience are able to evoke such a range of emotions, as quickly, and as dependably, as music. Granted, many one-nighters and bar gigs either don't have a decent sound system or people on staff you can count on to hit the damn "play" button when you ask them to. But 99 percent of the clubs you're ever going to perform in *will*. It's there for you, so why not make the most of it? Coming onstage to the right sound can set a tone for your act *before you've even opened your mouth*.

I can't tell you how many times I've watched a tired-sounding crowd come alive to the right song. In fact, I always travel with a cassette tape with over a dozen different intro songs. That way, as people file into the club, I can see whether the crowd is young, old, working-class, or artsy, and choose my intro music accordingly. Obviously I only use songs I like, but from such a collection, why not walk on the stage to a song I think the crowd might enjoy too? As always, it's about finding stuff that not only you like, but they like too.

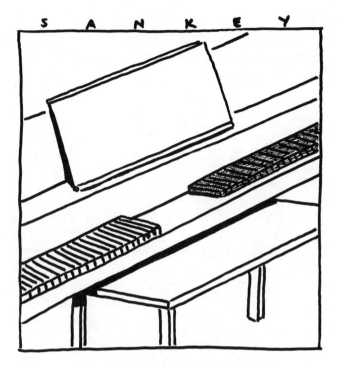

SOUTH AFRICAN PIANO

And don't think you have to limit yourself to "songs." There are so many distinctive sounds in the world. Imagine coming onstage to the sound of crashing cars, or submarine sounds, or barking dogs, or whatever. Something that sets you apart and wakes up the crowd. Experiment, but always keep your character and the tone of your material in mind.

As for using music in your actual routine, once again the so-called stand-up purists won't be impressed, but in my experience, audiences are usually thrilled. Remember, if you're the headliner, the crowd has probably already watched well over an hour of "guys telling jokes." Sure, you can go up there and tell more jokes too, and if you profess to be a stand-up comic you should certainly tell some. But if, along with telling funny jokes, you can use music in a way that also makes them laugh, it can only work in your favor.

CHAPTER SIX

SET STRUCTURE

God is in the details.

—Mies van der Rohe

Structuring a stand-up set is not unlike building a brick wall, with each joke being one of the bricks. You must not only carefully choose the bricks, but you must also carefully design the arrangement of the bricks to create a strong, trustworthy wall. And just as it is more challenging to come up with a design for a large wall than a small wall, it's more challenging to come up with a structure for a long set than a short set.

TO SEGUE OR NOT TO SEGUE

A segue is the means by which a comic goes from one joke to another—the thing that somehow connects two separate jokes. First, let me say that segues are definitely *not* always required. Perhaps many years ago, when stand-up was more akin to storytelling, the transitions between the stories were very important. But modern stand-up comics, with their short set-ups and even shorter punchlines, often jump from joke to joke with little or no noticeable segue. It's much more stream-of-consciousness, where things leap from subject to subject, often without having any apparent connections. Also, living in such a television-dominated society, with its unending cycle of quick cuts and commercial breaks, audiences are completely comfortable experiencing a barrage of seemingly unrelated information "bits."

But to my mind, just because people are comfortable with a series of unconnected information, it doesn't follow that they don't enjoy a presentation of *connected* information. In fact, I believe they enjoy it even more, and that on some level people find the experience of interrelated information more satisfying.

There are many, many ways of going from one joke to another while keeping a sense of connection or continuity. And just as a chain is only as strong as its weakest link, the more effective your segues, the more effectively your string of jokes will hang together.

SUBJECT MATTER

Arranging and connecting your jokes by their subject matter is probably the most obvious and most often employed means of segueing. Essentially, if you've got nine different jokes about raspberries, group them all together, usually with the last joke being the strongest. An exception to this rule would be if one of the jokes was a one-liner or a "throwaway," in which case you may well want to end your raspberry chunk with that. Going from joke to joke with the primary connection being subject matter usually results in a stand-up set made up of five or ten different subjects, depending on the length of the set. (Incidentally, if you do in fact, have nine different jokes about raspberries, get some professional help.)

EMOTIONAL THROUGHLINES

This is another common segue technique. Putting together five jokes about stuff that turns you on or three jokes about stuff that pisses you off or two jokes about stuff that makes you happy. Lumping your jokes together based not so much on similar subject matter, but on *your character's similar feelings* about the jokes.

MISTAKES

An actor doesn't think, he does.

—Sanford Meisner

The comic stumbles on a word and, in response to the apparent goof-up, goes into a joke. Or he drops the microphone, and then makes a joke out of that. Segues that require you to apparently make a "mistake" are particularly fun and challenging to perform. They can add an air of freshness and spontaneity to your set while also suggesting that you have a truly quick wit and can think on your feet. Crowds tend to really like this stuff.

SITUATION

"Finding" a hair on your sleeve, commenting on a logo on someone's T-shirt in the audience, saying something funny about the curtain on the back of the stage, or saying a joke about pretty much anything that is "there and then." Commenting on stuff like this in a humorous fashion almost always plays well. In fact, assuming that it's at least a little bit funny, you'll be surprised how well a crowd will respond to something that's obviously not part of your usual routine. I believe audiences appreciate, consciously or unconsciously, the apparent risk you're taking. It's just such stuff that makes you look like a real pro.

IT JUST OCCURRED TO YOU

This is sort of a non-segue segue, and is pretty much all in the delivery. You've just finished a few minutes about some subject or other, you take a sip of water, and then suddenly, as if it "just occurred" to you, you quickly launch into a question or blurt out a statement, which essentially is a set-up to yet another joke. But you deliver it as if it's truly right off the top of your head. Yes, in a sense, everything you say onstage should seem unprepared, but in this case, you say it with such *suddenness*, it seems even more unplanned than usual.

YOUR FIRST JOKE

All things considered, this is probably the most important joke of your set. Not only can it be very effective in setting a tone, but it can also go a long way toward establishing your character. If the crowd really enjoys your first joke, if they decide that you are, in fact, very funny, you've established trust that will stand you in good stead throughout your entire set. A successful first joke also relaxes both you and the crowd, making for much better communication.

But if they do *not* find your first joke to be funny, you are now in a position where you are going to have to make up for lost ground. So you would be wise to choose your opening joke, as well as the handful of jokes that follow it, *very* carefully. It's often a good idea for your opening joke to have unusually broad appeal. For instance, the chances are you would be better off choosing a joke about drinking beer than about fifteenth-century farming equipment.

Also, keep your first joke short. As much as long, involved set-ups are to be generally avoided, this is particularly so with your opening joke. Get to the laugh. After you take the stage, your goal should be to get to that first laugh as soon as possible. Incidentally, it is because of this idea of opening with a joke with broad appeal that many a comic's first joke will be about something in the news that day. Other performers will make a point of always trying to open with a joke about the city in which they're performing or even about the comedy club itself. But this is so commonly done, it can easily come across as hackneyed and unoriginal.

Stay Interesting

Let's say your first few jokes have done well. You've established a bit of your perspective, as well as made the crowd laugh. They trust you, they believe in you, they are listening to you, ready to laugh. But now that you've got them, you must keep them. One of the ways to do this is to stay consistently interesting. Think for a moment about those two words—"consistently" and "interesting." The first suggests the idea of repetition and uniformity, the second of engagement and stimulation. So at a very primary level, to keep a crowd's attention a comic's performance must somehow have a uniformity about it as well as be perpetually surprising. No simple feat.

VARY YOUR SUBJECTS

More often than not, the most engaging comics not only talk about a wide variety of things but also talk about these things in a wide variety of ways. They don't just do forty minutes of one-liners or forty minutes of impressions or forty minutes of jokes about quilting. They talk about a lot of different things. That way, if a certain percentage of the crowd isn't into one subject, they'll be interested in the next. It's also a good idea to present material that expresses a variety of different rhythms and structures. If all your jokes are approximately the same length, with approximately the same number of tags, it can create an effective rhythm, but it also can grow tedious, especially in longer sets.

EMOTIONAL RANGE

Just as it's generally a good idea to cover a variety of subjects, it's also a good idea to explore a *range* of emotions. To keep people truly interested, don't just talk about things that make you mad—talk about things that make you happy, sad, excited, curious, etc. Yes, you may well want to focus on one or two emotions or emotional themes (Dangerfield's "I get no respect" or Kinison always screaming) to leave the crowd with a definite impression of your character. But it is also a very good idea to be able to cover a rich range of feelings in that character. This ability will serve you particularly well in tough gigs.

NEARING THE END OF YOUR SET

Now's the time to really pick up the energy. Ideally, you want to end with a bang, generate the kind of crowd reaction that the audience, the management, and any agents in the crowd remember for a long time. It's not the time to try out new material. Instead, try to move into bits with several punchlines and several tags. Pieces that, over the months and years, have grown in size and power so that they really go and go. That way, the crowd will experience a building sensation. But keep in mind that you don't want any long applause breaks, not now. Instead, you want to keep the crowd's (hopefully) passionate response bottled-up so that, at the end of your set, they really let it go for you.

Many comics tend to do their rougher stuff nearing the end of their set. Watch some of your favorite comics; if they do some dirty or graphic or powerfully provocative material, they will probably do it closer to the end of their sets than the beginning. This is for several reasons. First, if they try it near the beginnings of their sets, before they've established a lot of trust with the audience, they run the risk of offending the crowd and the crowd getting off the bus. But later in their sets, after establishing themselves as talented, funny people, comics run less of a risk of losing the audience over provocative material.

More provocative material, if it plays, will often get a louder, more powerful audience response. So, there's another reason they keep that stuff until near the end. Note that I say "near the end" instead of *at* the end. I remember a young female comic in a comedy competition and, not as her last joke, but as her *second to last joke*, she did this very graphic bit about oral sex. Funny, but definitely blue. It got a very strong reaction, then she quickly closed her show with a safer, cuter joke. I can't remember whether she won the competition, but I do recall she did very well and several people commented on how clean her act was. She had done a very clever thing, not *ending* with a dirty joke, which would leave the crowd with a last impression of her as a blue comic, but putting it right near the end, to really goose the audience's final response.

YOUR LAST JOKE

Just as first impressions are very important, so are *last impressions*. And just as your first joke must establish you as a truly funny individual, your last joke, ideally, should leave a very strong impression in the minds of the audience that they were in the hands of a real comedic talent. Like your first joke, your last joke *must* be very strong. Many comics try to close on jokes that they know will get applause breaks. That way, when they then say "Good night," the applause simply builds from there.

It's also a good idea to always have more than one "last joke" ready. Several times I've seen a comic deliver their last joke, their tried-and-true blockbuster closer, only to get a soft response. And man, can it throw a comic. But you mustn't let it get to you. As always, the thing to do is to be prepared. Have another very strong joke ready to go.

But this can be a dangerous game, searching for that last big laugh to close with. Sometimes it just doesn't come, and while you're up there looking, time is ticking by, and you've probably done more than your fair share of time, and at that point you're just slowing the whole show down. So always try to have more than one closer in mind, but if it's just not coming together, the most professional thing you can do is to accept the situation for what it is, thank the crowd, and get off the stage.

YOUR SET

SHORT SETS (OPENING SPOTS)

These spots are between five and ten minutes long, usually early in the show. No matter how funny you are, there's little or no chance of tiring out the crowd, so you can go all out from the moment you hit the stage. Don't hold back or spend several minutes warming them up. Hit them between the eyes with your first joke and try to take the energy of the room upwards from there.

MEDIUM SETS (FEATURING OR MIDDLING)

These sets are usually between fifteen and thirty minutes long. Variety and modulation are definitely important. If the crowd isn't with you, thirty minutes can feel like a long, long time. Also, if your first fifteen or twenty minutes are very strong, there *is* a chance of tiring out a crowd. This is especially true if you try, from the moment you take the stage, to go all out. Typically, even very strong comics try to plan for at least a few minutes of slightly quieter laughter during a thirty minute set. They plan for this during sections of their sets where the material, though still strong, is not quite as powerful as much of their other stuff. Obviously, you don't want this lower energy or "catch their breath" section to be at the very beginning or at the very end of your set. Some comics plan for this break at the halfway point, and other comics do it just before their last ten minutes of killer material— a brief calm before the final storm.

Long Sets (Headlining)

These sets are usually between forty minutes and an hour. The best words of advice I can give is to quote an old stand-up saying, "If short sets are a fifty-yard dash, headlining is a marathon." If you are headlining a show, *everything changes*. First, since you are the last person on the show, the comic whose name is on the marquee, the crowd is going to grant you the most trust, give you the most room to, in a sense, do what you want. They assume (not always rightly) that you are the funniest comic on the show, so even if you start your set slowly, they know "it's coming." In fact, I have seen a few headliners really just kick around onstage for the first fifteen or twenty minutes before getting into it. Not a lot of laughs, some chuckles, chat with the crowd a bit, nothing much, and then start to pick things up.

This can be a good way to let the crowd catch their breath and cool off a bit if the opening acts have been very strong, and it can also be a subtle way of letting the crowd see just how comfortable and confident you are by not grabbing for laughs right off the top of your set. However, I prefer to establish that I'm funny within a minute or two of taking the stage, make them laugh hard for five or ten minutes, and then back off and shift down. That way, I figure, rather than the crowd having to take it on faith that I am funny, I have proven it *before* I do any casual cruising onstage.

But make no mistake, forty-five minutes is a long, long time. Very few comics can make a crowd laugh *hard* for that long. For a young headliner, it is tempting to hit the stage and "burn'em up" from the top and go, and go, and not let up, and go and . . . they get tired . . . and you glance at your watch . . . and you've only done twenty-nine minutes . . . and you've got at least sixteen minutes to go . . . and your show crawls to a close with some chuckles and short laughs, but also with a general sense of anticlimax. Avoid this by planning for periods in your set where you push them and periods where you let them breathe a bit. Plan your peaks and valleys.

When headlining, variety is more important than ever. Variety of the subject matter of your material, variety of the rhythm and structure of your jokes, and variety of the emotional range your character explores. I know more than one comic whose onstage character is really into the expression of one emotion in particular (anger) and what is very entertaining and funny for five or ten minutes becomes tedious and annoying after twenty. It's ironic but nonetheless true that the very characters that are so interesting and successful during short sets sometimes fail during longer sets.

This also applies to the *form* of your individual jokes. I know of one big-name comic in particular whose jokes are all pretty much the same length, the same rhythm, and express the same perspective, and while he will kill for fifteen or twenty minutes, after that the crowd grows weary of the repetition. They start to be able to see the jokes coming. It's one of the classic frustrations of the craft that, in attempting to develop a simple, unique, and memorable style, every comic runs the risk of being too easily categorized or becoming uninteresting after a short period of time. That's why the real goal is to create a character and a style that is *interesting enough*, and somehow *real enough*, that it's not only unique and marketable, but also able to hold a crowd's attention for longer than a four-minute TV spot or an eight-minute comedy festival spot.

I also believe that with longer sets it's a particularly good idea to try to work the stage, moving around, staying interesting to watch. If you're only doing five or ten minutes, standing there like a post telling jokes is fine. But to me, if you're going to try to entertain a crowd for close to an hour, one way you can remain consistently interesting is to use your body and the stage as much as possible. I don't mean jump around like an idiot, I mean intelligently, *purposefully* support your material with your hands, body, and your use of the stage. Comics with experience as actors tend to do this much more effectively than traditional comics. Headliners also sometimes try to incorporate something extra into their shows whether it's the playing of a musical instrument, an improvisational bit, or a dance number. As much as these kind of things are looked down upon by traditional stand-ups and so-called purists, audiences never fail to appreciate them.

GREAT SETS

When you do something, you should burn yourself completely, like a good bonfire, leaving no trace of yourself.
—Shunryn Suzuki

The crowd is laughing at your set-ups, exploding at your punchlines. People are laughing so hard they're wiping tears from their eyes. You can hear some of them actually coughing and struggling for breath. Some comics call it "killing," some call it "being in the groove," but whatever you call it, you're having a great time and absolutely everything is coming together.

The details of this kind of experience vary, but most comics agree that it feels like you can do no wrong. There's a powerful cohesion to your material, your character, your timing. In fact, the comic experiences everything so seamlessly, there's almost nothing for the memory to hold on to, which perhaps is why some comics say they don't remember much about really hot or great sets, they just remember having an exhilarating time.

When I've had a great set, I come off the stage feeling lighter, giddy, but also spent. Like I brought my raw ingredients onstage (character, script, energy) and the crowd brought their raw ingredients into the club (expectations, the need to laugh, life experiences) and when we met and mixed the ingredients together, something truly powerful happened.

Distinctions and divisions vanished; I had no obvious sense of myself as "the performer" and of them as "the audience." We were one vital thing. I find this seamless union more than a little ironic, considering that, as I've already mentioned earlier in the book, I think that the primary spirit of a joke is division, contrast, a *breaking* with presumption and convention. Perhaps it's through the sharing of these stark breaks that the comic and crowd arrive at a heightened sense of unity and sharedness.

CHAPTER SEVEN

AUDIENCES

Art is myself; science is ourselves.

—Claude Bernard

Meeting an audience is always a little like a blind date. They don't know you, you don't know them. Perhaps you've heard some good things about each other, but that's about it. When you take the stage, it's the very beginning of the relationship. Sometimes, the two of you hit it off from the very start and it's wonderful. Sometimes you don't quite understand each other and the date only goes so-so. And sometimes . . . well, sometimes it ends in a fight. You just never know, not for sure, until you're actually onstage delivering your material.

There are a lot of different kinds of audiences. Small and quiet, large and rowdy, uptight, mean spirited, you name it. And though there are some general rules when it comes to relating to an audience as a stand-up comic, to make the most of a situation, professionals often approach various audiences and venues with slightly different performance attitudes.

A Fish on the Line

I've heard actors refer to their relationship to an audience like having a big fish on the end of a fishing line. When fishing, the line runs from the fishing rod, disappears into the water, and the fisherman feels the pull of a strong fish, hooked on the end of the line, swimming somewhere down below. If the fisherman fails to give out enough line, the line may grow too taut and then suddenly snap, with the fish getting away. But if the fisherman gives out too much line, not only will the fish swim too far from him but the line may also get snagged on something and break, once again freeing the fish.

The fish is like an audience, the fisherman like a performer, and the line between them *the connection*. The performer is forever encouraging and nurturing. If the performer is too controlling and the connection becomes inflexible or brittle, it may well snap, and the audience will be lost. And if the performer is too casual, failing to assert himself and expend a concentrated energy, even an initially "caught" audience may grow distant from him and eventually get away. As with all things, success lies in a sensitive, responsive balance.

Leave Yourself Someplace To Go

The Law of Stimulation suggests that if a certain degree of stimulation isn't getting the desired response, you may well have to use *less* or *more*. In other words, some kind of change or shift is needed. Parents talk about hesitating to reprimand a child harshly because, the chances are, next time they're going to have to be a little harsher to make any kind of impression.

With stand-up, it's often safer to shift your energy *down* rather than *up*, because that way you leave yourself "someplace to go." Before you can afford the luxury of trying not to lose a crowd, you must first get them. This is why many young comics try to hit the stage with guns blazing, giving their maximum energy. But . . . if it doesn't work, if the crowd remains unimpressed, the comic has no place to go but to *lessen* his energy. To an unimpressed crowd, this can look a lot like defeat, and you can lose them. This is why, whatever the situation or crowd, think twice before expending too much energy too soon. Remember, if you start slowly, you can always speed things up.

SMALL AUDIENCES

Fewer than fifty people in the audience. As a group, they often feel self-conscious about their small size, and as individuals the people often feel exposed and vulnerable. Some comics go onstage and act like they're working a room of 400 people. This is often a mistake. With a small crowd, a comic is usually more successful if he delivers his material in a more intimate, conversational fashion. More than ever, make the crowd feel like a part of the show. But if you sense they are quite intimidated by their small size and would really just rather watch you do your thing, stick closely to your material rather than chatting with the crowd. But keep in mind, if you've got some jokes that, generally, only a handful of people really enjoy (as do we all), you better hope to hell that handful is among the people in front of you. Odds are they won't be, so you may want to skip your more esoteric stuff.

LARGE AUDIENCES

An audience of 200 or more. While small crowds are often like puppies and need to be dealt with gently, large crowds are more like big dogs. They like it when you play rough. Make sure to really project your voice and body to the back of the room. And work the *whole* room, not just the people straight in front of you. Keep swinging your focus from one side of the room to the other, connecting with everyone in the room. And remember, the more energy you give to them, the more energy they will give back. Now is also a particularly good time to try your edgier stuff, jokes that only a third of most crowds enjoy, because with 300 people, at least 100 people will be laughing . . . hopefully.

HOT AUDIENCES

The three comics before you all killed. The crowd laughed hard and long at everything, and you're up next. As always, there are several ways you can approach the stage. If you are doing a relatively short period of time, you may want to go up there, hit them hard right off the top, essentially "ride the wave" of what's already been established. On the other hand, let's say you're headlining, doing forty minutes or so. That's a long, long time to make a crowd laugh like crazy, especially after they've already been laughing hard for a solid hour. So you may want to go up there, establish trust with a really strong first few minutes, and then immediately back off, giving the crowd a chance to catch their breath, before then heating things up again.

COLD AUDIENCES

Zen is simply a voice crying, "Wake up! Wake up!"
—Maha Sthavira Sangharakshita

Two comics have already been onstage, and the audience, though large and apparently friendly, are not laughing much at anything. Has someone tried to talk to the crowd rather than just do material? If not, try it, and then slowly move into some material. If the act before you was pretty quiet and low key, try the "wake-up call" approach, going onstage and being loud and large right off the bat. Or if the comic before you was fast and loud, but still didn't get them, you may have better success by taking the stage with a more low-key approach, starting off casually and then slowly warming things up. This is not unlike making a camp fire. Some bark and twigs, then some sticks, then the small logs, and finally the big stuff.

The key with a cold, quiet crowd is to break the pattern of whatever the other comics before you have done. Not just when it comes to tempo or stage presence, but also with material. If the other comics have been getting little from the crowd with blue material, try starting with some squeaky clean stuff. "Calling the situation" can also work when you find yourself in front of a cold crowd. Try to get some laughs by calling attention to the fact that the crowd is hard to please.

Then again, sometimes the best thing to do with a quiet crowd is to take the stage and try to deliberately burn through your first ten minutes of material in six minutes, trying to wear down the crowd's resistance and pull them into the show with a fast-paced rhythm. Then as they perk up, gently slow it down to a more manageable speed. Cold crowds are one of the reasons why it is often a good idea to make a point of watching the act onstage before you, just to get a read on the crowd.

Joke-to-Joke Audiences

Some crowds are neither hot nor cold; rather, they spend the whole show judging each and every joke on its own, individual merits. They don't cool off, but neither do they ever seem to get caught up in the show. This isn't much fun for the comic. Sure, he's not bombing, but he senses the crowd will be with him on one joke, and then off the bus on the next. Perhaps the best thing to do with a crowd like this is not to push it, and just be grateful they get into some of the jokes.

Timid Audiences

Not only did the act that went up before you bomb, but he also took it out on the crowd and took the time to individually insult everyone in the first two rows. Now what? The crowd has probably lost a fair bit of faith in the entire show, so the first thing you must do is some-how *reassure them*. I think it's unprofessional to make a neg-ative comment about another comic while onstage, but if some jerk has just put the whole show in jeopardy, I think you owe it to the crowd to try to patch things up, even if it seems you are being slightly disrespectful of the other comic. So take the stage and right off the bat try to let the crowd know things are going to be different. Give some power and respect *back* to the audience.

WHY DO SOME AUDIENCES GET OFF THE BUS?

You had them for ten minutes, they were laughing at most of your stuff, and then . . . they seemed to cool right off. What happened? Well, barring a plague outbreak in the club, there's a good chance something you did damaged your credibility, you failed to meet an expectation, or you somehow offended them—you challenged them in a way they experienced as threatening or unpleasant.

Maybe you did a few bits that broke with everything you had done up to that point, and they simply stopped believing you. Maybe you had the MC give you an intro that gave the impression you were the "Funniest Guy in the Universe," and after your first few bits the crowd decided you couldn't live up to the hype. Or maybe you asked them to stretch too far too soon; you hadn't built up enough trust to safely go into your "tap-dancing leper" bit.

So they got off the bus, without even politely ringing the bell at their stop, leaving you to drive on alone. It's ironic because one of the reasons many people come to a comedy club is for *the experience of being challenged*, of having their usual lines of defense tested. But this has to be done in just the right way, usually in a playful fashion, and only after they've really come to trust the performer.

WHY DO SOME JOKES STOP GETTING LAUGHS?

You've been doing a certain joke for weeks, or even months, and all of a sudden audiences just stop responding strongly to it. Why? Well frankly, it could be any one of a number of reasons. Perhaps the joke is more character driven than idea driven, requiring you to perform the joke with an unusual amount of commitment for it to work. Bored with the joke, you no longer have the emotional energy it needs. Or maybe there was something subtle you weren't aware of that was always adding to the joke, and then one night, without realizing it, you stopped doing it. A facial expression, emphasis on a certain word, even the placement of the joke in your set. These can all significantly affect the strength of a joke. Or maybe the joke makes reference to information that finally became too obscure or dated. After all, there was a time when everyone was telling jokes about Julius Caesar.

SPRITZING

If your mind is empty, it is always ready for anything and it is open to everything.

—Shunryu Suzuki

"Spritzing" has to be one of the most magical words in the world of stand-up comedy. Essentially it means "saying stuff that is at least partially, and often fully, unprepared." This is not the same as stuff that, however casual it may appear, is actually a routine part of the comic's performance. Instead, to truly spritz is to actually talk off the top of your head.

This is usually done when talking with people in the audience about what they do for a living, if they're married, how many kids they have, etc. Some very wonderful comics are absolutely horrible spritzers, but most seasoned comics are pretty good at it. Then there are those comics who are master spritzers, seemingly able to somehow find the funny in the twinkling of an eye, in almost anything tossed their way. A little clever spritzing can go a long way toward gaining the trust of a crowd, and many of the strongest sets I've ever witnessed have involved at least a bit of spritzing. Few things bind the comic and the crowd more closely than *the funny things they find together*. That's the power of spritzing.

But it does have its downsides, or at least its limitations. In the moment, spritzing is king, but unlike strong material, lines and ideas that have worked in a thousand different situations, very little stuff a comic spritzes smoothly translates over into other shows or other mediums like film and books. This is probably because, more than any other aspect of stand-up comedy, spritzing is about the present relationship between the particular comic and the particular audience, on a particular night. Often, as wonderful as a line is, it will never again get the reaction it did on that one night. Oh well, that's performance art for ya.

BEING AN MC (MASTER OF CEREMONIES)

Over the years, I haven't done a lot of work as an MC, but I do know that it's a tough job. You are the first person to take the stage, the first face the crowd sees, and it is up to you to warm them up, to make them feel like they came on a good night, to acknowledge any birthdays or celebrations that may be going on in the club, and, finally, to prepare the minds of the audience to be receptive to stand-up material. And you have to do all of this despite the fact that many people are under the misconception that "the first guy is never funny." Sure, sometimes this is true, but in my experience, not only are MCs usually pretty funny performers, they are often *funnier* than the other acts on the show! But MCing is so tough, they seldom get the full credit and recognition they deserve.

Another challenging aspect of being an MC is the fact that, unlike the other performers who each get between twenty and forty-five minutes of uninterrupted time to develop their character, deliver their material, and establish a rhythm, MCs often only get short blocks of time onstage, during which they also have to make announcements and introduce the other acts. This is one of the reasons why comics who do a lot of work MCing rarely cultivate an offbeat or unusual stage character—they don't have the time to fully explore the character with the audience. Being the first comic to hit the stage and, in a sense, set a tone for the entire show, it's absolutely essential that an MC's character appeals to *a very broad demographic*. This is why the vast majority of effective MCs strive to come across as simply fun, friendly guys.

It's a very difficult job, maybe too difficult. In my experience, between talking to the crowd, spritzing, and giving attention to birthday parties, many MCs either fail to deliver enough real stand-up *material* to sufficiently prepare the minds of the audience for the first comic (who often ends up having a slow start as a result) or MCs do more than their fair share of time to compensate for all the time they have to spend with the birthdays, etc. It's a very hard job, and my heart goes out to them, but I don't think the answer is to steal time from the other comics.

INTROS

An MC will usually ask the other comics on the show what they'd like him to say about them. If I were you, I would give this some serious thought. Unless you are a well-known comic, what the MC says about you onstage will literally be the *very first impression* the crowd will have of you. Before you take the stage, even before your music, your introduction or "intro" will send a message, however, subtle, to the crowd. Make it count.

My first advice is to keep it brief. The MC has enough on his mind without trying to remember the names of your four different television show appearances, your film cameo, and the title to your one-man show. One or two credits is ample. Also, if you ask an MC to list a lot of credits, this can really raise the expectations of the crowd, expectations you may have a tough time living up to. Why put yourself under that kind of pressure? So keep it brief. Once again, less is more.

I also don't put much stock in funny intros, even if one does nicely set up your character: "Ladies and gentlemen, your next act used to be a 'boy toy' on a Norwegian fishing boat . . . ." Many MCs don't like prewritten, jokey intros, so they will often say them in a sardonic, glib, sarcastic, or even dismissive fashion, which can send a confusing message to the crowd.

To my mind, the best intros communicate the message that the comic about to take the stage is an experienced, funny person, well worth watching. That's it. Nothing more, nothing less. Anything else, I would much rather communicate to the audience myself during my performance.

EXTROS

This is whatever the MC says about you after you've left the stage, and the applause is just dying down. Most of the time he simply says, "Keep it going for . . . ," or "Another round of applause for . . . ," but sometimes, MCs say something a little more specific. Because I play a somewhat eccentric character onstage, MCs often extro me with, "That's one strange guy," or "Jay is available for children's birthday parties." This is fun, but I've seen some MCs extro comics with comments that were less than flattering and, frankly, unkind. To me, this is completely unacceptable. If you're ever the MC of a show, despite whatever differences you may have with another comic, I certainly hope you'll remain professional. I personally don't think negative comments about another comic are *ever* justified, no matter how big a laugh they may get.

HELL GIGS

Bars, outdoor shows, lunchtime shows at colleges. All of these situations have a real potential to get ugly. Generally, they will require you to give out a lot of energy, to keep people's attention by maximizing your stage presence. Such a challenge can be a very good thing, but as a result, these gigs are often not the best places to break in new material. If you lose the crowd on a new, somewhat soft bit, you might have a tough time getting them back. That's why I tend to see these gigs as a place to work out my *performance muscles*, rather than my writing muscles.

And tough gigs are also a great place to work on your emotional control, not letting your anxiety or doubt get the best of you. So much about performing is about trusting yourself. Hell gigs can be a fine place to work on that. And after you've worked a string of tough gigs, you'll find that it's a real treat to perform in a comedy club, with a good sound system, real stage lights, and a focused, enthusiastic crowd. Incidentally, seasoned pros try their best *not* to assume an audience will be difficult before they actually step onstage and begin their sets. Even if the comics before you have had a tough time, try to hope for the best for yourself or you may well limit your success with a negative attitude. Remember, crowds are strange, fickle things.

TOUGH CROWD

BARS

You're in a really noisy, smoke-filled bar. There's no stage, not much light, and you're simply standing on the floor with a mike in your hand. You asked for a mike stand, but you were told a bouncer broke it last week, beating a guy to death. You have to shout into the mike, almost eat the damn thing, to get any decent volume on your voice. And still, nobody's listening. They're playing pool, watching a football game on a big television screen (management warned that if they tried to turn it off there *would* be a riot), and a drunk guy sitting in the front row is loudly singing to no one in particular. It's a hell gig.

These crowds are often pretty drunk and boisterous, but also usually quite friendly. The key is to be bold and take control from the very beginning. Let the local funny guy have his say, and then get on with the show. Doing some stuff with local references (to a nearby town, say) can really endear you to this kind of crowd. And it's often a good idea to keep your material pretty simple. I don't mean stupid or crass, just don't expect your wry, gently ironic stuff to kill.

Lighting is often pretty bad in bars, so don't expect to get much reaction from your "cross-eyed butcher" impression. Think ahead and, if a bit really requires the crowd seeing a certain facial expression to nail the joke, you may want to consider dropping it from that night's set. Use your voice more, your face less.

OUTDOOR SHOWS

This includes picnics, summer parties, or pretty well any situation where you have to perform outdoors. First, these often happen during the day, and as a general rule, it's tougher to make people laugh when the sun is up. Oh, you can do it, and sometimes you can even do very well, but because most people work during the day and their recreational time is at night, it seems that they are simply more receptive to being entertained after the sun's gone down.

Also, being outside, most of the sound systems you'll come across won't be good enough to carry the subtleties of your voice to everyone in attendance. So it's a matter of performing to those within earshot. If they can't hear you, those interested will simply move closer to the stage. And working outdoors, sometimes under a hot sun, be prepared to sweat. Make sure you have a glass of water and a handkerchief, or at least a neatly folded paper towel.

NOONERS

These are lunchtime or afternoon gigs held at colleges, universities, and occasionally high schools. They can be a lot of fun, but they *do* have a lot of things going against them. First, there is almost never a cover charge to see the show. The school is paying, so the students get in for free, and whatever people get for free they often don't think is worth much. As a result, the students often don't exactly exude respect for the performers and are apt to sit at a table, right in front of the stage, playing cards or holding an algebra study group. Second, the shows are usually held in the cafeteria. Students are forever coming and going, and everyone is trying to wolf down some food between classes. Not the best environment for intellectual focus. And again, these shows are held during the day, so the "it's harder to make them laugh during the day" rule applies.

Another reason a nooner at a college is often much harder than a *night show* at a college is because night shows tend to be held in the student bar with everyone in a much better mood to relax and have fun. Or they hold night shows at an on-campus theater, which can be a real pleasure to work in. And night shows tend to have some kind of cover charge, so the students are more apt to try to enjoy the show and get their money's worth.

SURVIVING HELL GIGS

Bars, outdoor shows, and colleges all have the potential to become hell gigs. But as always, there are several things you can do to at least *try* to make them go a little more smoothly.

GET MANAGEMENT INVOLVED

Try to minimize potential distractions *before* you take the stage. If you're working a bar, approach the manager with a positive attitude and ask if they could maybe turn off the televisions or the lights over the pool tables. Or if there isn't much stage light to speak of, even turn off a couple of the lights at the *back* of the room to give the stage area a little more focus. Make these requests in a casual but firm manner. Making these kind of requests also applies when working in a college cafeteria.

But don't act like the success of the show hinges on management adapting the situation to meet your needs. Instead, act as if, "We're going to have a fun show no matter what, but here are a few things we can do to make it even better."

TAKE CONTROL

This is very important, particularly in potentially difficult situations. From the moment you take the stage, you must *immediately* establish yourself as a powerful individual and capture the crowd's attention. Now's the time to "play large," really project, and own that stage. You must be absolutely fearless. And don't wait for them to come to you. When you're headlining at a comedy club you can take your time. But a really tough gig can be like a street fight between you and the crowd. Generally speaking, whoever swings first and *connects*, wins. Take your show to them. Your character, your jokes, your energy. All of it.

DON'T YELL

Try not to yell. This is tough not to do, especially if the sound system is really bad. After all, even more important than being able to see your face is for them to be able to *hear* you. But yelling or straining your voice is only going to suggest to the crowd that you're anxious and not in control. Often, the best thing to do is to project your voice to the best of your abilities without straining it, and then simply accept the limitations of the sound system. In fact, some performers *deliberately* speak more quietly in such situations in hopes that it will force the crowd to quiet down so they can hear what the comic is saying. Unfortunately, this doesn't always work.

ADAPT YOUR MATERIAL

Softness triumphs over hardness. What is malleable is always superior over that which is immovable. This is the principle of controlling things by going along with them, of mastery through adaptation.

—Lao Tzu

If you're working a blue-collar bar, don't open your set with your wry "Kierkegaard in a Traffic Jam" bit. If you're gigging outdoors for the Society of Catholic Gardeners, don't close your set with your "Papa Beelzebub" chunk (no matter how life affirming you think it is!). And when working colleges, keep in mind that they are, after all, college kids. An awful lot of them are mostly interested in passing exams, drinking beer, and getting laid. So make fun of algebra, talk about partying, and close your set with your "Papa Beelzebub" chunk.

PLAY TO THE LISTENERS

Some people, at some gigs, are simply *not* going to listen to you. They're too drunk, they're having an important conversation with a friend, they're doing some last minute studying for an exam, they don't much like stand-up comedy, whatever. So hey, it isn't your job to force people to listen to you. Hell, strictly speaking, it isn't even your job to *coax* people to listen to you. Your job is to tell jokes and make anyone who wants to listen to you . . . laugh. So play to the people who are listening to you, and try to ignore the people who are not. And as always, try not to take it personally. More often than not, it's not about you, it's about them.

HECKLERS

Be nice, until it's time not to be nice.
   —Patrick Swayze in the movie *Roadhouse*

DON'T ASK FOR HECKLERS

Whether at a comedy club or a bar gig, sometimes all it takes is one guy with a bad attitude or a chip on his shoulder to ruin a show for everyone. But why do some comics get a lot more hecklers than others? I figure it's because something about their onstage characters attracts hecklers to them. Some comics seem a little disrespectful of the crowd, other comics seem unsure of their own abilities, and still other comics deliver material about sensitive subjects in an overly cavalier fashion. Any and all of these things can diminish the crowd's *primary respect* for the performer, virtually inviting hecklers. So while you develop ways of dealing with hecklers, also put some thought toward not encouraging hecklers in the first place.

However, you have a definite responsibility to everyone who paid to listen to you, and if some loudmouth is undermining the quality of the show, it's up to you, the professional, to do something. Here then are some suggestions, in order of severity, the idea being that you try each one while dealing with a heckler, then go back to delivering your material. But if the heckler persists, move on to the next suggestion.

GIVE HIM SOME ATTENTION

Some guy at the back of the room just shouted something. You're not quite sure what he said, but you figure it probably wasn't "You're an amazing comic!" So give him some attention. Find out what he said, get his name, maybe even find out a bit about him. This often does the trick, because hecklers usually just want a little attention.

LET HIM (OR HER) KNOW YOU HAVE A SHOW TO DO

He's still shouting stuff. Gently comment that you've "got to get on with the show." A surprising amount of people who go to watch stand-up comedy think that the comic *wants* them to shout things out, to give the comic "something to deal with." There are lots of subtle and not so subtle ways of telling hecklers, "Thanks, but no thanks." But beware of hitting too hard, too soon. Nothing can turn off a crowd faster than if you come across as a bully.

One show I did, a guy in the front row just kept talking and wouldn't shut up. I gave him some attention, then backed off. Then, five minutes later, I gently zinged him a few times, then backed off again. But he *still* kept talking. I admit, I let it undermine my concentration, as well as get to me emotionally, and I finally let loose with a string of hard-edged put-downs. Big mistake. The majority of the crowd didn't know the guy had been talking nonstop. I hadn't "cued them" to this fact, so I ended up looking like the big jerk.

SEND A JOKE HIS WAY

You've been patient, nice even, but enough is enough. Precious minutes are ticking away, and if he's not going to shut up you're going to have to assert yourself and give him a rap on the knuckles by making him the butt of a quick, not too harsh, insult. But don't linger on it. It's essential that, at this stage, you still give him a chance to back down and save face. And remember, as you deal with this guy, continue to inform the crowd; "I can't believe it, he's still talking!" It's crucial that they understand your motivation.

GET THE CROWD INVOLVED

As I said, if it's someone in the front row and most of the crowd can't hear him, be sure to keep cuing the crowd to what's going on. But after a point, it's also fair game to *subtly* coax the audience to help you deal with the heckler. You do not want to look like you need help or are in the least flustered. As a stand-up comic you must look like you are in *complete control*. If you ask the crowd, "By applause, how many people here paid to listen to this guy shout incoherent stuff?" the vast majority of the time the crowd will quickly support you.

SHUT HIM DOWN

It's time "not to be nice." Deliver a couple of your harshest, strongest insults. Show no mercy. He had his chance, you gave him some warnings and plenty of opportunity to save face. But as always, do not deliver them with anger or too much passion. That can suggest a lack of confidence to the crowd. I also find that the more clever or imaginative the insults, the better. The cleverness acts as misdirection from the true intent of the barb: to shut up the heckler, once and for all.

BOMBING

Whoever thought silence could sound so loud? You've tried everything. Slowed your delivery down, sped it up. You've tried talking to people in the crowd, tried squeaky clean material, quickly shifted to some rawer stuff . . . but absolutely nothing is working. The silence just continues, getting more obvious and awkward every moment. You're exhausted, you feel like you're moving around onstage with large, heavy stones in your pockets. You can actually feel the crowd's boredom and frustration. They don't think you're funny. Hell, at this point, *you* don't think you're funny. You are bombing. But believe it or not, there *are* some things you can do, attitudes and techniques that can definitely help.

DON'T LET THEM KNOW YOU'RE BOMBING

The crowd is always looking to you to see how they should feel about what you are doing. It is absolutely essential that you keep this in mind at all times. When a child falls on the ground and a parent is nearby, the child often looks to the parent to get the parent's take on the event. If, instead of looking alarmed or frightened, the parent smiles or seems unconcerned, the child will often get up without bursting into tears. So if you're bombing, as hard as it can be, try not to let the crowd see your disappointment or anxiety. Even as you're saying, "Shit, shit, shit" inside, try not to get flustered. If you don't let the experience get to you, if you act like everything is going along pretty much as planned, you'll be surprised how smoothly a bad show can go. I'm not saying this will fool them into thinking you are incredibly funny, but it *can* make the difference between them thinking "He was terrible" and "He was alright." And at some hell gigs, that can be a real achievement indeed.

CALL THE SITUATION

If you find yourself in the middle of a performance that is going very poorly, don't fight it! It's going to happen. That's what learning is all about. So try not to let it unnerve you. That will only make you start to sweat and do stuff that will signal your panic and desperation to the crowd. In fact, when bombing, some comics have great success with a technique that is the *exact opposite* of the "don't let them know you're bombing" approach. Instead, these comics "call" the situation, and admit to the crowd that the set isn't going quite as well as they had hoped it would, and often this diffuses some of the tension in the room. Keep in mind that sometimes, when one finds oneself feeling weak, admitting to it can be very self-empowering.

Calling the situation can also be very, very funny. I know comics who have developed so much material *about* doing badly that they often seem to deliberately start to bomb, just so that they can go into their "I'm bombing" material. But this can be very dangerous. Not only can it backfire on the performer with the crowd simply agreeing, "Yeah, you *do* suck," but it can also be a real creative trap. You won't always have the time to lose a crowd and then get them back. Television spots, festival appearances, and many other situations require that you do well, ideally *very* well, in less than seven minutes. Sometimes in less than five. So though I think it may not be a bad idea to have some "I'm bombing" material, I think it makes even more sense to continue to strive toward being able to do well in every room imaginable.

BASE HITS VS. HOME RUNS

The less effort, the faster and more powerful you will be.
—Bruce Lee

Another way of dealing with bombing involves *changing your delivery*. If you take the stage and start delivering material that usually gets big laughs and it's getting nothing, you may want to immediately consider changing not only your delivery style but also your degree of commitment. Try delivering the stuff a little less "large"; tone it down a bit. Don't get caught swinging your bat like you're trying for home runs. Instead, deliver like you're trying for a base hit, swinging the bat less broadly, less emphatically. Remember, it's never a good idea to give an audience the impression that you are wanting, reaching, or asking for something.

And if that's not working, if they still aren't even chuckling, well then, maybe back off on the delivery *even more*. I don't mean drop to your knees and start quietly mumbling your jokes, just try saying them in an even more casual, conversational style. Try bunting a few jokes, or even acting like you're just fiddling with the bat, feeling its weight, tapping it against your shoes. Standing onstage, just loosening up.

ACCEPTANCE

As soon as one cherishes the thought of winning the contest or displaying one's skill in technique, one's swordmanship is doomed.

—Takano Shigeyoshi

This isn't so much a helpful technique as it is a liberating attitude. I remember when I used to bomb on amateur nights. Some shows I was so bad, and the crowd reaction was so harsh, I would feel it in my stomach for days. I just wish I knew then what (I believe) I know now. Simply that, you will be doing both yourself and the crowd a big favor by accepting the following fact: *Not everyone will always love you.* Wanting every crowd to enjoy your work is a fine motivator for you to work hard on your craft, but I believe it is also absolutely critical for you to be able to accept the present limitations of your material and character, wherever you happen to be along the road of your own personal growth.

For example, if at some point in your exploration of comedy, you are only interested in doing material about your summer as a librarian at a Bible camp, and you find yourself in front of a bar full of drunk bikers, chances are you're not going to have an amazing set. Yeah, I personally like the idea of striving toward having a comedic perspective, rich enough and broad enough that I can do well in *any* room, no matter the age or cultural background. But I can't honestly say I'm there yet. In fact, I kind of like the idea of never quite *arriving* there, of always believing I'm on my way—maybe even getting closer all the time, but not ever absolutely arriving. It's an attitude that both inspires me and gives me room to breathe.

EVERYBODY BOMBS

If they aren't laughing, I find it hard to breathe.
—Brian Regan

I consider Brian Regan to be one of the funniest comics I've ever seen, and yet I once saw him perform at a big comedy festival, in front of a crowd filled with television executives, and he *bombed*. I mean, really bombed. It was not pretty. And like I said, Brian Regan is a phenomenal comic. So remember, everyone bombs. Everybody. Sure, as you get more experienced you bomb less. But you still have the occasional "soft set." Many times since seeing Brian Regan bomb, I've thought about the fifteen years he's been in the business, and about how important that show could have been for his career, and about how deserving a comic he is, and it reminds me that sometimes no matter how good you are or how hard you work, things don't always come together when you want them to. That's life, and one can either accept it or one can vainly fight against it. I figure, when you bomb the best thing you can do is try not to take the experience too personally. Remember, it's not the end of the world. Learn what you can from it, and then forget about it.

CHAPTER EIGHT

PROFESSIONAL STAND-UP

SELF-PROMOTION

Inspired self-promotion can have a very positive effect, not only on your career but also on your craft. After all, it's a simple fact of the business that the more time you spend onstage, the better a comic you will become. And the more effectively you promote yourself . . . the more opportunities you'll have to get onstage!

NEVER BELIEVE YOUR OWN PROMO

This is of paramount importance. Yes, your promo should be based on the *truth* of your experience, comedic style, and achievements, but it should also be presented in such a way as to appeal to *other people's imaginations*. I'm not saying make stuff up or even distort the things you've really done. But I do think it's definitely a good idea to present the truth about yourself in as positive and engaging a light as possible. Remember, it's show business. I guess that's why the word "hype" often has a negative connotation to it, because in powerful promotion materials there is often an element of theater or drama that, taken too far, can become downright manipulative and deceitful.

One of the dangers of exaggerating your abilities and achievements is that you run a real risk of "overselling" yourself. Then when it comes time to perform, you fail to meet the expectations you yourself created! So by all means, appeal to the imaginations of potential decision makers (agents, bookers, producers, festival organizers, etc.), but try to think of your promotion as a kind of performance on paper. Another, perhaps even greater danger of taking your own hype too much to heart is that if you think you're "God's Gift to Stand-Up," you may well stop pushing yourself creatively, which is nothing short of *artistic suicide*. Just as when you blame the crowd for a bad show, if you believe your own promo you give your ego a chance to grow irresponsible and lazy.

A UNIQUE TYPE OF COMMUNICATION

Almost every aspect of the craft of stand-up involves the idea of communication, the conveying of specific information to other people. The area of self-promotion is no different. In fact, during your entire career, no money will ever be better spent than the money you spend on your promotional package. Imagine for a moment walking into some office, and the receptionist has her feet up and is on the phone with her boyfriend. Makes for a very bad first impression of the business, doesn't it? Your promo package *is* your receptionist, and will sometimes be the very first impression important decision makers will have of you. It's no time to be thoughtless or cheap.

AIDA

I spent a couple of years writing for advertising, and though I can't say it was a particularly pleasant experience, I did learn a lot about persuasive communication. One of the most important things I learned was the "AIDA Rule of Communication," for *Attention, Interest, Desire, Action.*

More often than not, when you are communicating with someone you are doing so with a goal in mind. You would like the listener to respond in a particular fashion, but to get someone, to respond to what you're communicating you first must get their attention. I mean, if they aren't listening, what's the point? So whether you are experimenting with your material, your character, or your promo, your first mandate is to always get the attention of your audience.

But you not only want to get their attention, you also want to keep it. To do this you must *create interest.* It's one thing to get their attention, but for your audience to even consider getting emotionally involved in what you are communicating, they must be interested. This is why, if you can, it is always a good idea to stay close to the things that naturally interest people.

As for the desire part of the AIDA Rule, this refers to the link between Interest and Action. Loosely speaking, "interest" is a relatively intellectual investment, but for someone to go so far as to act, they also must be involved emotionally. Along with interest, you must also *create a desire* in the audience. One means of doing this is to make the audience curious. If they are curious, they are not going to be merely interested in what you are saying, but they will also have a desire to hear what it is you are going to say. More than anything else, it is that desire that will cause them to act—in other words, to make a real effort to listen to you.

Applying these ideas to your marketing material, you ultimately want to design a promotional package that:

1. gets people's *attention*
2. creates *interest* in your stand-up
3. causes them to *desire* to see or speak with you
4. causes them to *act* by calling and booking you for a show.

YOUR PROMOTIONAL PACKAGE

When discussing character, I suggested that you try to write up a short list of words that best describe your personality onstage, e.g., cerebral, sedate, etc. These words will also be very helpful when it comes to putting together your promo package, because every single piece of your package should reflect a *similar style or tone*, ideally that of your character and comedic perspective. So when trying to choose a color of paper, a typeface, or anything else, keep your character's key words in mind, and do your best to have your choices reflect a similar sensibility. For example, if your character is bookish and insightful, choose an academic-looking typeface. If your character is a bit crazier and off-the-wall, choose a more eccentric typeface. But beware the temptation to try to be funny in your package. More often than not, it comes across as strained and actually works against you.

LETTERHEAD

I suggest that whatever ink color you choose, stick with a high-quality white paper. But try to have some fun with a custom-designed letterhead. Just your name is fine, but you may want to have a slogan or just the word "Comic" as well. Apart from my name, I also have a little logo on my letterhead. It's the same logo I have on my stickers (and I also have a rubber stamp of it). I just like the idea of having an image, other than my own face, that is repeated throughout my promotional material, to tie it all together that much more.

BIOGRAPHY (OR "BIO")

This is often the first page of a package, listing your television, radio, and festival credits. However, if you are quite new to the business and don't have any such credits, you can simply give some background information on yourself—if not as an experienced comic, at least as an interesting person. But as always, try to keep it as original and engaging as possible.

This page should also have a paragraph giving a brief description of the basic style and tone of your stand-up. Again, if you have a short list of key descriptive words about your character, it will certainly come in handy.

QUOTES FROM THE MEDIA

You don't need dozens of these, four or five will do just fine, reproduced in bold lettering on a single sheet of paper. And rather than have them all say similar stuff, try to choose a small collection of quotes from articles that express a variety of different views about your work. A quote about your energy, one about your clever writing, one about how experienced you are, etc.

NEWSPAPER ARTICLES

Ideally, these should be articles written solely about you, rather than articles in which you are merely one of many comics mentioned. But in cases like that, you may want to cut out the paragraph pertaining to you, enlarge it on a photocopier, and then reproduce it, with the title of the article and the writer's name, on a single sheet of paper. Incidentally, though colored paper can look nice in a promo package, when it comes to copies of newspaper articles, I would stick to white paper. It's easiest to read, and sometimes agents and bookers will want to make copies of articles from your package, and black ink on white paper reproduces best.

PHOTOS

If you can afford it, have two or three different pictures. One for comedy clubs, and another one or two for casting agents for commercials and film work. In the comedy club photo, you should look professional, friendly, interesting, and if at all possible, funny. Stick to black and white, rather than color, if only because newspapers want black and white. And again, the goal is to have a photo that somehow stands out from the thousands of dull, boring, typical photos you see on the walls of comedy clubs across the country. Have some fun. How about a photo of you leaning up against a police cruiser, being frisked by a huge cop? Or sitting in a laundromat staring at the dryer? Or hitchhiking? Try to do something memorable. Remember, in show business, *the biggest risk is not taking any risks.*

As for your photos for casting agents, you have to be a little more careful. Attractiveness is a real factor, and they look at a lot of small details. Your eyes, teeth, hair, all play important parts. The best thing to do is call a casting agent you've heard good things about, ask him or her to suggest a photographer, and get some pictures done. Then call the casting agent back and ask for *five minutes* of her time. Show her the photos and ask for her honest opinion. Listen very, very carefully, and take everything she says as the absolute gospel. She is, after all, your "target market."

POSTCARDS

This is one of my favorite pieces in my promo package. An intriguing photo of me on one side, and plenty of room to write stuff on the other. I send them to agents when I'm on the road (saying "Hi"), which at the same time leaves the impression that I'm busy and in demand. And if I'm doing a special show, I use my postcards as invitations, with the time, date, and place of the show printed on self-adhesive labels I stick to the postcards. Postcards aren't cheap, but if you buy them in a large quantity, they aren't overly expensive. And if, like me, you tend to move every year or two, I suggest you don't have your phone number or address printed on the cards. Just your name and logo.

FOLDER

As soon as you have more than a couple of pieces to your package, you will need something to put it all in. I find that the classic cardboard folder, plain on the outside, two large horizontal pockets on the inside, is just fine. Mind you, it won't hold your video, but I just slip that, along with the folder, in a large, padded envelope.

MAILING LABELS

I have self-adhesive, two-by-three-inch labels with my letterhead on them. I find they have a lot of different uses apart from putting them on letters, envelopes, and packages. For example, I stick them on my demo tapes and on the cover of the folder that holds all my promo materials.

STICKERS

I also have small, self-adhesive stickers with my name and a small logo printed on them. These too have a lot of uses. I stick them on the backs of envelopes, the bottoms of letters, and on photos. Again, it's little details like this that can separate you from the pack, while also giving the impression of quality and success: "If the guy's got money to spend on little stickers, he must be doing well."

VIDEO

Again, less is more. Agents and producers rarely watch more than a few minutes of a tape, which is why many comics use tapes five to ten minutes long. Tapes of a TV appearance, dubbed from Beta to VHS, are ideal, but even a high-quality videotaping of a strong club set is better than nothing. However, if you can't afford a high-quality taping, I suggest you *do not include* a tape in your package. The last thing you want is a tape that, instead of enhancing your image, actually tarnishes it.

THANK-YOU CARDS

After a week at a club, or if a newspaper prints an article on me, or pretty much whenever someone in the business has done something nice for me, I always, always send a thank-you card. And it never fails to amaze me how often I hear back from them that they seldom receive such cards! They're a strong marketing tool and leave a lasting impression, yet very few comics seem to bother to make the effort to send them. To me, this is not only ungrateful but also a real self-promotion mistake.

PROMOTIONAL EVENTS

RADIO INTERVIEWS

These can be a lot of fun, whether done live in the studio or over the phone. Typically, interviewers are looking for you to be funny on air, so *be prepared*. One way to do this is to give the interviewer a short list of questions he or she can ask that will "naturally" lead you into some of your bits. Humorous poetry, songs, or other stuff you can read off also tends to play well on radio. And be sure to have a list of key points you want to make during the interview: where you're next performing, the dates, times, the phone number people can call to get tickets, etc.

FUND RAISERS AND BENEFIT SHOWS

"They'll be lots of media there, and we'll even feed you." That's what they'll tell you, time and again, when you're booked for a fund raiser or a "freebee." And though they will give you dinner, don't count on there being much media. These shows generally go alright, but the crowd certainly won't be pumped or primed for the joke-to-joke rhythm of stand-up. And usually the crowd will be made up of a lot of older people, often quite conservative, so you should probably keep your material pretty clean and accessible. Also, be sure to find out the theme of the fund raiser or the group you're raising money for. The last thing you want to do is open your set with your kooky "kidney failure" bit, only to later discover it was a fund raiser for PWOKA (People With One Kidney Association).

Comedy Festivals

When putting together a set for a comedy festival, there are two classic approaches, very much depending on your objectives. If you want to get booked into other comedy clubs, you'll probably want to choose a group of jokes that express a single, *concentrated* character and perspective. The goal, as always, will be to be memorable. However, if your goal is to impress television people, you might better go with a set that gives you a chance to show a *variety* of abilities, from tight writing to acting to pacing, etc. Of course, these two approaches are not mutually exclusive, but like an advertisement that tries to appeal to too many different target markets at once, if you try to do too much in a six-minute festival set, there's a real chance of failing to leave a distinctive impression with anyone. And just like when performing on television, at a festival you should probably stick to tried-and-true material that you've been doing for months, if not years. The odds are you'll be nervous enough as it is without having to worry about new material.

Stand-Up Comedy in the Age of Television

There's little doubt that the proliferation of stand-up comedy on television has played a large part in the steady decline of attendance at comedy clubs over the last ten years. But I also think that comedy clubs have changed. I suspect that audiences once came to clubs expecting that not only would conventions be challenged and provocative perspectives be expressed, but also the performers would do truly memorable things. In those days, they weren't just shows, but actual "happenings." And yes, the days of relatively naive audiences in awe of comics may well be gone, but I don't think that has to signal the end of the popularity of stand-up comedy. It may simply mean *we have to change.*

I for one believe that "we shall overcome," that we can woo people away from their television sets, but only by performing stuff people can't see on television. It's that simple. If people can sit on the couch at home and watch any number of comics on television standing behind a microphone telling one joke after another, I figure we have to do something other than simply stand behind a microphone telling jokes. Something more, something different. "Like what?" you may ask. Good question.

We must make the most of the live performance situation. It's an indisputable fact that a live performance can be *much* more engaging and powerful than a television show, but it's up to us as performers first, and comics second, to make our shows *more powerful and engaging* than the tired, uninspired, unoriginal, stand-up crap they can watch on television. We have to make every effort to make our audience members feel involved in the show. This is something the "watch me" medium of television has a more difficult time doing.

PERFORMING ON TELEVISION

Leave your ego at home. A television appearance invariably involves dozens of creative people, and they all want to feel like they've had a say in the final product, so be prepared to have your feelings bruised. Also, if you're an unknown, be prepared to have relatively little creative control. But thankfully, many of the people you will be working with (though certainly not all) will have a *much* better idea of what works on television than you do. So you do your job, and let them do theirs!

As for clothes, it's always a good idea to bring a few different sets of clothes and ask for opinions from the wardrobe people. And during your set be sure to have a glass of water handy, especially for your first few television appearances. The last thing you want is to get a dry mouth due to nerves and not even be able to finish your performance.

Not surprisingly, most television tapings will require you to work squeaky clean. No swearing, and often not even any perverse subject matter, like your recipe for fresh raccoon Jell–O (with that nutty, furry taste!). And instead of doing five minutes on one subject, you may want to cover a *variety* of subjects in your set. That way, if the studio audience isn't enjoying one subject, chances are they will be interested in the next. And be sure to avoid jokes involving callbacks to previous jokes. The final edited version of the show may not even contain the joke you were calling back to!

When delivering their material, many pros make a point of delivering their set-ups to the studio audience, and their punchlines to the camera . . . Yes, the hundred people in the studio matter, but not as much as the thousands of people watching at home. Those are the people you really want to make laugh and leave with a strong impression. But all things considered, the most important thing about a television appearance is getting some strong footage for your promo reel. The appearance itself may go to air once, maybe even a few times, but your promo reel will eventually be seen by dozens of important decision makers. This is why, instead of having a buddy tape the show on his VCR, do absolutely everything you can to get a *broadcast quality* tape of the show. It will make for a much better transfer.

And finally, really watch your time. On television, every second costs tens of thousands of dollars. If the director says you have four and a half minutes, he doesn't mean four minutes and forty-five seconds. The show may even be running long by the time you get on, and they may have to cut to a commercial before you've finished your set. That's why comics with a lot of television experience often make sure they can end their set with any one of their last three jokes, just in case.

YOU, OTHER COMICS, AND THE AUDIENCE

Despite the fact that most comics are lone wolves (maybe, in fact, *because* of this), most comics want the respect of their peers. Sometimes more than they want the respect of their audience. But everything costs. Art making, the nurturing and exploring of one's own unique vision, can be very lonely work, but it can also be immensely satisfying and self-empowering. I sometimes even think the more power one gives to others, the less power one keeps for oneself.

Put another way, the more value you put on other people's opinions, perhaps the less value you put on your own. That can be a very dangerous thing, especially for an artist. So though I think we can all definitely learn from each other, I also think it's very important *not* to put a great deal of importance on the views of other comics, especially when you consider that all people can ever share with you is their prejudices.

On the other hand, I believe that valuing the *views of the audience* is absolutely essential. Like the tango, it takes two for a truly great show, with both you and the crowd playing your parts to the best of your abilities. You must trust each other and get a sense that you really care about each other's feelings. Only under such conditions can a stand-up performance become a happening.

WHOSE ADVICE SHOULD YOU TAKE?

Do not seek to follow in the footsteps of the men of old; seek what they sought.

—Basho

Listen *first* to yourself. Only you know what you're after and what feels right to you, and as scary as it can be to trust yourself and really risk falling flat on your face, there is no other way, not if you want to get to the unique stuff that really makes you who you are.

Listen *second* to the audience. As their partner in the experience, I believe the comic must also pay the utmost attention to the crowd's response. Not only will they tell you in no uncertain terms (laughter or silence) what they enjoy and what they don't, but they will also tell you a great deal about many of the audiences you will encounter in the future. After all, the reason a great show works is because the performer is somehow exploring not just his own fears and fantasies, but the audience's as well. That's why a successful stand-up performance is more akin to group therapy than individual therapy, with both the performer *and* the audience benefiting from the intensity of the shared, cathartic experience.

And listen *third* to anyone who is where you want to be. Other people will forever be offering you advice, especially when you first get started. Comics will have advice on jokes, waiters and bartenders will have advice on stage presence, agents will have advice on how to promote yourself. There is never any shortage of people with advice. But I figure the people to really listen to, perhaps the only people you should pay any heed to, are the people who are living a life you yourself would like to live. So you may want to think twice before following the advice of a comic who still isn't headlining, even after ten years in the business. Unless of course you want to one day be where he is—still not headlining, even after ten years in the business!

Just as some people say one of the keys to becoming wealthy is to socialize with wealthy people, I believe you should search out those individuals who are where you want to be and put a great deal of stock in what they say. And I don't just mean comics or even other performers. I find I get a lot of inspiration listening to or reading about almost any artist or thinker whose work I find to be powerful and engaging. So instead of taking to heart the negative, self-aggrandizing advice of some bitter local "pro" comic, or the advice of some overly opinionated relative, only listen to those people whose hearts and minds you truly respect and admire.

COMPETITION

The way of the sage is to act but not compete.

—Lao Tzu

Stand-up can be *very* competitive. Every night, several comics vying for the adoration of one crowd. And though

I believe a certain amount of friendly competition between comics can be healthy, I also try to keep the following in mind . . . Sometimes, when driving for hours traveling from one town to another, I'll find myself passing this car or that truck. And then a little while later, if I have to pull into a gas station to fill up, I'll think of the cars I passed on the road and how, now that I've pulled over, the chances are I'll have to pass them again. And for a moment, I feel a little frustrated. But when I really think about it, I figure my sense of frustration or anxiety is based on an illusion. On the road I'm traveling, I've covered the miles I've covered, and nothing or no one can take that away from me.

TROUBLE IN THE PLAYGROUND

DRUGS, ALCOHOL, AND SUPERSTITION

Many artists jump into the waters of their art wearing a life preserver, and more often than not, it's the life preserver that drowns them.

—Henry Miller

Some comics like to drink booze, some like to smoke drugs, and some like to always leave the TV on when they leave the hotel room or always wear their lucky shirt onstage. Of course, each to his own, do what you believe, but I try my best not to invest too much belief in anything *outside myself*. Actually, I figure being a comic is very much about being the most "me" I can be, and about investing as much value in my own perspective as possible.

I believe absolutely everyone has a unique perspective, but very few people are encouraged to explore it, let alone express it. More often, people seem to be urged to empower ideas and institutions outside themselves, which I think is really a subtle form of superstition. To me, this is the danger of using drugs or alcohol or food or whatever *to excess*. What's "excess"? Well, I figure we all answer that question for ourselves, but the moment you experience your involvement with something as restrictive or inhibiting rather than liberating, the chances are you're using it to excess.

Another problem with looking for power in people and things outside oneself is that it's tough to really count on. And stuff like dope and alcohol have a definite "best before" date on them. Sooner or later, they tend to catch up with comics. Mind you, in some bar gigs, taking a beer onstage with you can make you "one of the crowd," and that can be a good thing. But *requiring* something apart from yourself and a microphone to be a funny performer makes you less flexible, and in some contexts you're going to pay the price.

The fact of the matter is, a good percentage of comics eat a lot of crap and drink a lot of booze. The personality types, the life style, always being around alcohol, the stress, the lonely nights. Living as a stand-up comic can be a very real personal challenge. But the way I see it, the sooner a comic learns to cope with being a comic *without* resorting to things that run a definite risk of eventually blowing up in his face, the better.

BURN-OUT

One minute I'm the best album of the year, the next I'm the worst thing that's ever been created on earth. So if I want to go on that roller-coaster ride, then I'm an idiot.
—Alanis Morissette

I've had many really rough nights, and after a few shows I care not to even remember, I have seriously considered giving it up. But one of the ideas that has given me the guts to stick with it is that every show is not so much an end in itself, but a *means* to something much bigger and better. Namely, *a funnier me.* Perhaps without even realizing it, the crowd has paid to come watch me . . . learn. Sure, there've been nights, especially back when I was still on amateur shows, when the crowd thought I was absolutely the worst comic they had ever seen. They didn't have to tell me, I could literally feel it, and sometimes continued to feel it, in the pit of my stomach, for days later. But I always tried to remind myself that, ultimately, I was struggling my ways toward a more creative, more expressive me (as I still am).

Then, when I got off amateur nights and started to get paid for shows, I kept telling myself that, unlike the majority of colleges and universities where the student has to pay to attend, I was *getting paid to learn*. Yes, every night you find yourself onstage, you should try to really be there for that crowd, but on an even more important level, whether the show goes well or not, it is merely a means to a greater end. Along the way, try not to take the potholes too much to heart. If only because, in show business, there tend to be a lot of potholes.

Rather than trying to get used to the extreme ups and downs of the business, I suggest you try to adopt a more accepting, even *gently detached attitude*, especially considering that, after years of ups and downs, it's not uncommon for a performer to feel burnt out. That's why, I personally try to look at it all a little more . . . philosophically, I guess. I try not to take the downs or the ups too seriously. Where I am is important, but so is where I'm going.

LULLS IN YOUR CREATIVE GROWTH

Having talked with many different kinds of artists, there seems to be a consensus that the longer one practices a craft, the harder one has to work to continue learning. As the years go by, the learning curve tends to flatten a bit, with the individual apparently learning less with each passing year than he did in the first few. One reason for this is that, in those first several years, everything is brand new and you are approaching everything with truly fresh eyes. You're hungry and there's so very much to learn. Not that, after you've been practicing an art for a decade or more, there's not much left to learn. On the contrary, more often than not, masters of a craft emphasize that one never knows it all—or anywhere *close to it*. But after several years of thought, practice, and study, many students of a particular craft find that, where in the first few years they seemed to always be automatically learning, now they have to push themselves to continue to grow. Stand-up is no different.

Lulls in progress, both artistically and careerwise, can be frustrating, puzzling, even depressing. But remember, it's at times like this that the hobbyists get out of the business, and the real, die-hard comics *hang in*. Do everything you can to try not to let it get to you. I've had many of these lulls at different points in my growth, and one of the things I keep asking myself is, "Am I funnier now than I was six months or a year ago?" Usually the answer is "Yes."

Keep taking the stage, keep trying new stuff, and even if you feel like you aren't learning much, it's almost inevitable that you will be getting funnier. And that's what it's all about. Yeah, agents, bookers, and key decision makers have a real say when it comes to the progress of your career, but you have most of the control when it comes to your artistic growth. *That's all up to you.* So, after four or five years on the boards, with a solid forty-five minutes of material under your belt, don't let up, don't stop pushing yourself.

But it isn't easy. Typically, seasoned comics become unimpressed with a certain degree of audience reaction and thirst for louder and longer laughs. The audience reaction they would have sold their souls for a few years earlier now leaves them feeling strangely dissatisfied. And that can be a good thing, if they respond to this feeling by pushing themselves harder to write and perform to the very best of their expanding abilities. The pattern is often one of the young comic having an unusually strong set. Then a year or so later, this unusually strong set is now the comic's usual set. Then some time later, he has an even stronger set, and a year or two later that is now the new standard for that comic. And so it goes. Be prepared for both the mountains and valleys. Odds are, as you progress as a stand-up comic, the valleys between the mountains will grow wider and sometimes (groan!) even deeper. But have faith. Keep giving of your heart and time to your craft, and with a little luck, another mountain will be yours.

BEING PROFESSIONAL

What does it mean to be "professional"? Well, unlike an "amateur," a professional often makes money, perhaps even his entire living, from what he does. But to my mind, that's probably the *least* important aspect of what it means to be professional. For me, professionalism is more of an attitude, even a code of behavior. Stuff like personal hygiene and punctuality I hope to hell I don't even have to mention, but there's also a lot of other, more subtle stuff. However, being such an individual thing, I'm certainly not about to suggest what being professional should mean to you, but here's at least a little bit about what it means to me.

DO YOUR TIME ONSTAGE

If the manager of the club asks you to do twenty-five minutes, do twenty-five minutes. Not eighteen, not thirty-four . . . twenty-five. It's that simple. If you're having a tough time and you want, really *want* to get the hell off the stage, but you're supposed to do another ten minutes . . . do another ten minutes. That's how you learn. And how you fulfill your commitments to other people. If you go short, somebody else will probably have to make up your time, and that's simply not fair. It's also not fair if you're having a blast onstage and, instead of the ten minutes you were asked to do, you do nineteen. There's a word for that—it's called "stealing." From the other comics, and from the crowd.

Stand-up is a craft of seconds and minutes, not hours. Some comics believe that a crowd can only laugh so hard for so long before they get tired. I'm not sure if I completely believe this, but I suspect there is at least *some* truth to it. So if you're a stage hog and stay onstage longer than your allotted time, strictly speaking, you're stealing from the other comics. And whether you're bombing or killing isn't the point. Also, if you aren't the headliner on the show, not only are you stealing from him (he's got a hard enough job as it is, trust me) but also you're stealing from the crowd who paid to see the headliner. And when you go long or bail early you aren't showing respect to the manager who has booked you to perform for a certain length of time.

TRY (TO THE BEST OF YOUR ABILITIES) TO MAKE THE AUDIENCE LAUGH

Yes, you want to explore that new "leprous insurance salesman" character, break in those salamander jokes, maybe even try that new marmalade bit, but you're being paid to make people laugh *tonight*. So as you try to grow, and you must, always try to make sure there's truly something in it for them. And yeah, some nights they may not go for what you call your "smart stuff," so try something else. I figure you owe them that. To not always necessarily succeed, but to at least always *try*.

DON'T TELL JOKES ONLY YOU (OR OTHER COMICS) ENJOY

To my mind, playing to "the back of the room" or for your own personal kicks can, once again, be summed up in one word: stealing. The people in the audience paid you to entertain *them*, that's the deal. If you don't like it, don't accept the gig. Many's the time I've heard comics onstage saying, "That's a joke I do for myself." Imagine a surgeon saying, "While I was stitching you up I put in a couple of stitches in your armpit, you know, just for myself." Or the club manager not paying you your full fee, explaining, "It's a little something I do for myself."

DON'T TELL JOKES AT THE EXPENSE OF THE STAFF OR OTHER COMICS

To me, this is inexcusable. Yeah, we all have our small grudges with this comic or that bartender, and yeah it's not much fun taking the stage after another comic has just bombed for twenty minutes telling one tampon joke after another. But if you have a problem with someone, that's between you and them. It's like parents fighting in front of the kids. I don't think it's fair to drag the crowd into it.

Now, I *can* think of one exception to this, but it's very tricky. I figure the people who come to see us perform are, on some level, our *guests*. Their pleasure is our first priority. So just as when someone has clearly been very rude or mean to a guest in my home, I may feel obliged to say or do something. In the same way, if a comic has clearly been very mean to someone in the crowd, perhaps, just perhaps, it may not be completely out of order for me to say something onstage or do what I can to make amends—if only for the sake of the entire show.

IF THEY DON'T LAUGH, YOU AREN'T FUNNY

Yes, last night you killed. And you may well rock the house tomorrow night. But tonight . . . well, they didn't laugh much. So I figure, tonight you weren't funny. It's not unlike that old question, "If a tree falls in the forest and nobody's there to hear it, does it really make a sound?" To me, to be "funny" is to be *found to be funny* by another person or persons. So if an audience doesn't laugh, you aren't funny, at least to them. It's not about being "too smart" or "too hip" for the room. Have you ever heard a mechanic say he wasn't able to solve a problem with a car engine because he was "too clever"? If you're so damn clever or smart or whatever else you call it, prove it and *reach the crowd in front of you*.

One of the ways I force myself to own up to certain

hard truths, particularly after a rough show, is by asking myself, "Can I think of a comic, *any* comic, who could've done more with that crowd?" And if the answer is "Yes" (and, considering comics like Robin Williams and Jim Carrey, the answer is always "Yes") then I am, once again, left holding the responsibility bag.

It's Never the Crowd's Fault

I can't tell you how often I hear comics blame the audience for a bad show. To me, that's like a teacher blaming her students for an unproductive class. We're supposed to be the pros, we're the ones getting paid, we're the ones who have done it hundreds if not thousands of times. We write the stuff, we deliver the stuff, we do it all. So I figure the buck should stop with us. Even when my ego doesn't like it, I always try to accept full responsibility for how my part of the show goes. They paid to see me, I have the mike and the lights, and they're facing the stage. Under those conditions, I think I should take full responsibility. Though I admit, sometimes it's not very easy or much fun.

Some comics will say this is taking things too far, that the audience as a whole has a definite say in the dynamic of the show, and I would agree. But I'm not suggesting you try to take full responsibility just for the sake of the audience, but for *your sake* as well. My ego (perhaps like yours) can be a very clever, sometimes slippery thing. And I believe that the fewer "exits" I give it, the more I'm going to push myself to become a better comic. Taking full responsibility for the audience's response to your set goes a long way toward blocking those exits.

ALWAYS BE LEARNING

Learn something from every shot.

—Cliff Thornbird
(world champion billiards player)

Push yourself. Don't rest on your tried-and-true forty-five minutes or your always charming character. The "greats" of almost any discipline or profession tend to think of themselves as amateurs, as students, forever trying to learn more about their area of interest or so-called expertise.

PAY YOUR DUES

Nobody gets great overnight. Nobody. Hell, nobody gets even really good in a few months. It takes years, accept it. Somebody once said it takes five to seven years to get good, truly good at something, and in my experience and that of a lot of people I've talked to, that's the truth. So don't make it hard on yourself (and everyone around you) by straining to be somewhere you are not. You are where you are. Enjoy it for what it is.

BE TRUE TO YOURSELF

To me, this is the most important of all. I know that many of the other aspects of being professional I've touched on emphasize the importance of honoring your commitments and obligations to other people. But what's the point of being fair to other people if you aren't being fair to yourself? So if you find yourself not being able to give others what you've agreed to give them, without also ripping off yourself, then perhaps stand-up comedy isn't for you. Or to put it another way, if you can't make a crowd laugh with the kind of comedy you want to do, and the kind of comedy you feel they might enjoy you don't feel comfortable doing, stand-up comedy may not be for you. For many comics, including myself, it's a never-ending struggle, sometimes quite fierce, between doing what you think the *crowds* might enjoy and doing what you think *you* might enjoy. They are seldom the exact same thing. That's why the most successful comics somehow find a way to be true to both themselves *and* their audiences.

CHAPTER NINE

ZEN and the ART of STAND-UP COMEDY

Flow with whatever may happen and let your mind be free. Stay centered by accepting whatever you are doing. This is the ultimate.

—Chuange-Tzu

I've always been a pretty anal guy. Punctual, wicked tidy, very controlled. But at times, that can be a frustrating, restrictive way to be. I mean, just because I tend to do things a certain way, it doesn't mean I'm always going to like it, right? As controlling as I sometimes am, for years now there's been a part of me that yearns to be a little more easygoing, better able to go with the *spontaneous flow of things*. I suspect it's this part of me that was first attracted to stand-up, and to the philosophy of Zen.

I can't claim to know a whole hell of a lot about Zen. In fact, from what I've read, "knowing" and "Zen" don't have much in common. But I'll tell you what the idea of Zen means to me, as a person, and as a stand-up comic: Zen is about staying open to the unexpected, and about the spontaneous nature of life itself. Zen is about flexibility rather than rigidity. Zen is about doing, whatever you do, with as much of *you* as possible. It's about being "in the moment," about really being where you are. And most of all, Zen is about investing all of you in what you do.

WATER IS STRONGER THAN ROCK

When I first started reading about Zen, I was excited to see so many parallels between some of the ideals of Zen and my own thoughts on stand-up. When Zen philosophers talk about water being stronger than rock due to water's profound flexibility, I'm reminded of the importance of staying loose on stage, and of not letting stuff like loud pinball machines and waitresses dropping trays of beer get to you. Instead of resisting or fighting such so-called intrusions, disregard them. Or perhaps even better, *incorporate* them into what you are doing. Exclusion, perhaps of any kind, is a very dangerous practice. Stay open, stay flexible. Make an ally of the Spontaneous and Unexpected.

YOU ARE WHERE YOU ARE

To rule Nature, you must first give into it.
—John Locke

When reading about Zen, I also find myself thinking a lot about Acceptance, about trying not to make something into something it's not. Perhaps like yourself, I've many times found myself in an unpleasant situation, a place I dearly didn't want to be. But *there I was*. And no amount of wishing or hoping or wanting or even needing was going to change the fact that, at least for the time being, that was where I was. A thing is what it is. A biker bar is a biker bar is a biker bar.

So instead of putting thought and energy into wishing for this or hoping for that, I now try to accept the situation for what it is, and put my energy toward making the most of the situation. I know, it's not exactly a new idea. But I personally am still trying to find what it takes to always do it.

FEAR IS THE ENEMY

Earlier in this book, I suggested that caring strongly about how your set goes, combined with a little self-doubt, will serve you in good stead. But that's as a beginner. Starting out, doubt and concern will push you to search and experiment with many important techniques. But I believe there eventually comes a time, a time when you are finally able to "snatch the pebble out of the teacher's hand," that you must begin to, in a sense, go out into the world . . . alone. Beyond the school walls, even

ZEN SKIER

beyond strongly caring about other people's opinions. Caring can be a great fuel, but it can also be a very real trap, especially if it is fear in disguise. Especially when you consider that the tightrope walker who thinks too much about falling often does that very thing.

Much of what people teach, including many of the principles I discuss in this book, are merely guides, suggested paths, all ultimately leading away from where they begin. After all, that's the nature of a path: to take you someplace else. Many of the things one learns before setting off on any journey will serve one in good stead for a long time to come, but I believe that as a performing artist, one of the things one eventually has to leave behind is fear of failure. I myself am not there yet. I still fear failing, fear not "doing well." But I am getting less fearful all the time. And I think that's a good thing, if only because I believe any fear I may have stands between me and The Moment. In a sense, between me and Me.

Don't Try (Or: Just When I Thought Things Couldn't Get More Confusing)

Zen suggests that one of the symptoms of the fear of failure is the idea of "trying," of somehow pushing or influencing or willing oneself to be something else. Instead of just being who you are where you are, when you are, and how you are . . . you *try*. I still remember the time it occurred to me that perhaps "trying is to doing, as training wheels are to a bike." I know, even to me it sounds pretty vague. I mean, how the hell am I supposed to "try not to try"? I guess by doing something else other than trying. Like what? I haven't a clue. But I do feel like I have a subtle sense of it. And sometimes, just for a second, I swear I even catch a glimpse of it. And so, I continue to think about it, and feel about, and yes, even write about it.

STRAINING/RESTRAINING VS. ZEN

First, I should point out that the above heading is, strictly speaking, a contradiction. As I've already mentioned, Zen as I see it is very much about inclusion, not exclusion. Put another way, about love, not fear. So to suggest that Zen is "versus" anything is to imply a fixedness or rigidity that I don't believe Zen has. (But hey, I'm trying to make a point, so cut me some goddamn slack!) Earlier in this book, I discussed the danger of the crowd perceiving the comic as in any way straining. His voice, his body movements, his temper, whatever. Strain often comes across as a sign of fear and insecurity, both of which can seriously compromise the comic's image in the eyes of the audience. I even went so far as to mention the virtues of being restrained onstage, and how that can send to the crowd a clear message of strength and confidence.

But now, to the ever-growing heap of different views, I would like to suggest a third perspective, one very much related to the idea of "not trying." Imagine yourself onstage delivering your material, and you're not straining (unnaturally pushing yourself) and you're also not restraining (unnaturally holding yourself in). In such a scenario, what then are you doing?

I'm not quite sure. I seem to have an easier time imagining strain, and restrain, than the total lack of either. But perhaps you are simply . . . being there, onstage, naturally offering to the audience whatever it is you are, in that moment. No sense of division between how you feel and what you do. No sense of division between your character and your material. No sense of division between *you* and the *audience*. I believe that too is Zen.

Twenty Tips

1. Smile.
2. Leave the audience wanting more.
3. Be flexible.
4. Simple is better than complicated.
5. Stage time is precious, don't waste it.
6. Play to the entire room.
7. Beware talking too quickly.
8. Remember, likable and vulnerable.
9. Commit fully to your material.
10. Variety is good.
11. Try to have fun onstage.
12. Always be professional.
13. Ask the audience for nothing.
14. Do your time, no more, no less.
15. Start strong, end strong.
16. Don't just express, communicate!
17. Tape your sets.
18. Don't wait for the audience to come to you. Go to them.
19. Keep writing.
20. Trust yourself.

The map is not the territory.

—Alfred Korzbybski

Glossary

Angle: a comedic perspective on a subject, also "spin" or "take."

Bit: a single joke on a subject.

Callback: a joke that makes reference to information contained in a previous joke.

Character: the personality or role a comic plays onstage.

Chunk: a series of jokes on a subject.

Closer: the last joke of a comic's set.

Conviction: doing something with great belief.

Commitment: investing a great deal of yourself in something.

Curiosity: interest in knowing more about something.

Extro: what the MC says about a comic after he leaves the stage.

Gig: an engagement, show.

Green room: a tiny room in a comedy club reserved for the comics.

Guest spot: a brief appearance on a show, often without pay.

Hack: one who tells common, unoriginal jokes.

Headliner: the last comic on the show.

Heckler: someone who disturbs the show, often by shouting insults at the comic.

Hook: an aspect of a comic's performance or character that sets it apart from other comics.

Intro: what the MC says about a comic before he gets onstage, e.g., his television credits.

Joke: something one says or does to make people laugh, also "gag."

Laughter: a release of tension in reaction to a surprise.

Material: jokes prepared before the show.

MC: Master of Ceremonies.

Opener: the first joke of a comic's set.

Prop gag: a joke with a prop.

Punch: information that alters the meaning of already given information in a surprising fashion.

Riff: unprepared comment.

Set-up: information that gives a joke an initial context and perspective.

Sight gag: a nonverbal joke.

Schtick: a comic's particular style.

Spritzing: spontaneously finding humor, often while talking to the crowd.

Stage hog: a comic who stays onstage longer than he is supposed to.

Surprise: something that happens without warning.

Timing: the tempo and rhythm of a comic's voice and actions.

Tag: a brief line said after the punchline.

Tension: a build-up of unreleased energy.

Zen: your guess is as good as mine.